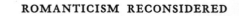

ROMANTICISM RECONSIDERED

Romanticism Reconsidered

SELECTED PAPERS FROM THE ENGLISH INSTITUTE

EDITED WITH A FOREWORD BY Northrop Frye

COLUMBIA UNIVERSITY PRESS   NEW YORK AND LONDON

Copyright © 1963 Columbia University Press

First printing 1963
Third printing 1966

Library of Congress Catalog Card Number: 63-18020

Printed in the United States of America

The essay by René Wellek has previously appeared in his *Concepts of Criticism* (Yale University Press, 1963) and is used here by permission of Yale University Press.

THIS BOOK consists of four papers read at the English Institute in September, 1962, under my chairmanship. The four contributions are entirely independent of one another, and whatever similarity there may be, such as the fact that the first three papers all quote the same passage from Wordsworth, is pure accident. Consequently the resemblances among them, and the unity which they present, is all the more significant.

The anti-Romantic movement in criticism, which in Britain and America followed the Hulme-Eliot-Pound broadsides of the early twenties, is now over and done with, and criticism has got its sense of literary tradition properly in focus again. That this movement should ever have had so much authority is an impressive negative tribute to the coherence of critical theory in our time. There are a few references to the movement in my own paper, which is intended to serve as a general introduction both to the topic and to the three papers that follow. But it was not the influence of this movement which was the main reason for holding a session on the subject of "Romanticism Reconsidered" at this date. The main reason was to examine the degree of real content which the term Romanticism has. It is a datum of literary

experience that when we cross the divide of 1798 we find ourselves in a different kind of poetic world, darker in color, so to
speak, than what has preceded it. Our initial attempts to define
the difference may be very vague: "more emotional," "more
sense of nature," and the like. At this stage, as Mr. Wellek re-
marks, an "extreme nominalism" like that of Lovejoy, in demon-
strating that there is no conceptual unity to the term Romanticism
at all, seems unanswerable. But the feeling of difference remains,
and critical theory has not done its job until it accounts for the
feeling.

Mr. Abrams's paper singles out one difference so concrete and
well documented that it is unanswerable evidence for the other
side. The Romantic movement found itself in a revolutionary
age, of which the French Revolution was the central symbol. The
impact of this event is testified to on all sides, and (as Mr. Abrams
remarked in the discussion afterwards) it is always a sound critical
method to assume that serious poets mean what they seriously
say. The fact of revolution was linked in many poetic minds with
the imminence of apocalypse—the association of ideas that Mr.
Abrams quotes from Coleridge as: "The French Revolution. Millennium. Universal Redemption. Conclusion." But the apocalyptic
word did not remain revolutionary flesh for very long: anticlimax
and disillusionment quickly followed. Mr. Abrams connects the
frequent later Romantic theme of the plunging of hope into
despair with this disillusionment, and shows that as the only
place in which hope springs eternal can be the human mind, the
theme of revolution fulfilling itself in apocalypse had to be trans-
ferred from the social to the mental world. The only part of the
mind to which such conceptions as revolution and apocalypse

belong is the creative imagination, hence Wordsworth's real revolution was a literary one, a "levelling" revolution in diction, and in the location of archetypes in common rather than heroic life. Such a feat was not a neurotic subjective substitute for revolution, but the articulating of a new kind of imaginative power—and also, of course, the bringing into literature of that new movement which we know as Romanticism.

The pattern of an outburst of enthusiasm followed by disillusionment is picked up again, and greatly extended, in Mr. Trilling's essay. Here the attitude of Wordsworth and Keats toward pleasure is seen as an element in the new consciousness of the central importance of the arts and of what they can yet do for man. The sense of the goodness of pleasure, even of a frankly luxurious kind, is part of the exuberance of individuality which is present in both poets. But the same thing happens to Romanticism that happens to Satan in *Paradise Lost:* the separation of consciousness from what supports it is exhilarating at first, and then restrictive. The individual becomes the ego, and the ego turns to a kind of perversion of puritanism, seeking the principle of its own being in a pure detachment which rebuffs everything that it might come to depend on or be indebted to, especially pleasure. The undying ego, whose rasping, querulous monologue enters literature with Dostoevsky's *Notes from Underground,* is a parody of what used to be called an immortal soul; and pleasure, so often thought of as a threat to that soul, turns out to be the most dangerous enemy of the ego, so that Wordsworth's conception of pleasure as "the naked and native dignity of man" is rejected but not refuted. Many features of Mr. Trilling's eloquent paper indicate that contemporary culture is post-Romantic, in other words still a part of what began with the Romantic movement.

Both Mr. Abrams's paper and Mr. Trilling's deal with central and essential aspects of the Romantic movement. Still, they could conceivably have been written without using the term Romanticism. The question still remains: Is this term a necessary or functional one for studies of what happened between the fall of the Bastille and our own day? The question cannot be answered until it has been properly asked. Poets work with images rather than concepts; hence an historical literary term, such as Romanticism, really belongs to the history of imagery rather than to the history of ideas in the sense of concepts or theses. Mr. Wellek's exhaustive and erudite survey indicates that attempts to define the term Romanticism have been successful in proportion as they have moved away from the dead end of Lovejoy's conceptual approach toward studying what the Romantics did with images and symbols, in their effort "to identify subject and object, to reconcile man and nature, consciousness and unconsciousness by poetry."

It is a hazardous enterprise to introduce three papers that one has not read, and my attempt at doing so was perhaps more fortunate than it deserved to be. Their main theses are to some extent adumbrated in my introduction. That Romanticism is primarily a revolution in poetic imagery; that it is not only a revolution but inherently revolutionary, and enables poets to articulate a revolutionary age; that as the noumenal world of Fichte turns into the sinister world-as-will of Schopenhauer, Romanticism's drunken boat is tossed from ecstasy to ironic despair—these are the chief points I make, and they are the ones so fully documented and analyzed later. At the very least, the editor can say with some confidence that there is enough which is both new and important in the present book to encourage the reader to reconsider Romanticism for himself.

N. F.

CONTENTS

ROMANTICISM RECONSIDERED

Northrop Frye

THE DRUNKEN BOAT: THE REVOLUTIONARY

ELEMENT IN ROMANTICISM

ANY SUCH conception as "Romanticism" is at one or more removes from actual literary experience, in an inner world where ten thousand different things flash upon the inward eye with all the bliss of oversimplification. Some things about it, however, are generally accepted, and we may start with them. First, Romanticism has a historical center of gravity, which falls somewhere around the 1790–1830 period. This gets us at once out of the fallacy of timeless characterization, where we say that Romanticism has certain qualities, not found in the age of Pope, of sympathy with nature or what not, only to have someone produce a poem of Propertius or Kalidasa, or, eventually, Pope himself, and demand to know if the same qualities are not there. Second, Romanticism is not a general historical term like "medieval": it appears to have another center of gravity in the creative arts. We speak most naturally of Romantic literature, painting, and music. We do, it is true, speak of Romantic philosophy, but what seems to us most clearly Romantic in that are such things as the existential ethic of Fichte or the analogical constructs of

Schelling; both of them, in different ways, examples of philosophy produced by an essentially literary mind, like the philosophies of Sartre or Maritain in our day. So at least they seemed to Kant, if one may judge from Kant's letter to Fichte suggesting that Fichte abandon philosophy, as a subject too difficult for him, and confine himself to lively popularizations.

Third, even in its application to the creative arts Romanticism is a selective term, more selective even than "Baroque" appears to be becoming. We think of it as including Keats, but not, on the whole, Crabbe; Scott, but not, in general, Jane Austen; Wordsworth, but not, on any account, James Mill. As generally used, "Romantic" is contrasted with two other terms, "classical" and "realistic." Neither contrast seems satisfactory. We could hardly call Wordsworth's preface to the *Lyrical Ballads* anti-realistic, or ignore the fact that Shelley was a better classical scholar than, say, Dryden, who, according to Samuel Johnson, translated the first book of the *Iliad* without knowing what was in the second. Still, the pairings exist, and we shall have to examine them. And yet, fourth, though selective, Romanticism is not a voluntary category. It does not see Byron as the successor to Pope or Wordsworth as the successor to Milton, which would have been acceptable enough to both poets: it associates Byron and Wordsworth, to their mutual disgust, with each other.

Accepting all this, we must also avoid the two traps in the phrase "history of ideas." First, an idea, as such, is independent of time and can be argued about; an historical event is not and cannot be. If Romanticism is in part an historical event, as it clearly is, then to say with T. E. Hulme: "I object to even the best of the Romantics" is much like saying: "I object to even the best battles of the Napoleonic War." Most general value-judgments on Romanticism as a whole are rationalizations of an agreement or disagreement with some belief of which Romantic poetry is supposed to form the objective correlative.

This latter is the second or Hegelian trap in the history of ideas, which we fall into when we assume that around 1790 or earlier some kind of thesis arose in history and embodied itself in the Romantic movement. Such an assumption leads us to examining all the cultural products we call Romantic as allegories of that thesis. Theses have a way of disagreeing with each other, and if we try to think of Romanticism as some kind of single "idea," all we can do with it is what Lovejoy did: break it down into a number of contradictory ideas with nothing significant in common. In literature, and more particularly poetry, ideas are subordinated to imagery, to a language more "simple, sensuous, and passionate" than the language of philosophy. Hence it may be possible for two poets to be related by common qualities of imagery even when they do not agree on a single thesis in religion, politics, or the theory of art itself.

The history of imagery, unlike the history of ideas, appears to be for the most part a domain where, in the words of a fictional Canadian poetess, "the hand of man hath never trod." Yet we seem inexorably led to it by our own argument, and perhaps the defects in what follows may be in part excused by the novelty of the subject, to me at least. After making every allowance for a prodigious variety of technique and approach, it is still possible to see a consistent framework (I wish the English language had a better equivalent for the French word *cadre*) in the imagery of both medieval and Renaissance poetry. The most remarkable and obvious feature of this framework is the division of being into four levels. The highest level is heaven, the place of the presence of God. Next come the two levels of the order of nature, the human level and the physical level. The order of human nature, or man's proper home, is represented by the story of the Garden of Eden in the Bible and the myth of the Golden Age in Boethius and elsewhere. Man is no longer in it, but the end of all his religious, moral, and social cultivation is to raise him into something resembling it. Physical nature, the world of animals and plants, is the world man is now in, but unlike the animals and plants he is not adjusted to it. He is confronted from birth with a moral dialectic, and must either rise above it to his proper human home or sink below it into the fourth level of sin, death, and hell. This last level is not part of the order of nature, but its existence is what at present corrupts nature. A very similar framework can be found in classical poetry, and the alliance of the two, in what is so often called Christian humanism, accounts for the sense of an antagonism between the Romantic movement and the classical tradition, in spite of its many and remarkable affinities with that tradition.

Such a framework of images, however closely related in practice to belief, is not in itself a belief or an expression of belief: it is in itself simply a way of arranging images and providing for metaphors. At the same time the word "framework" itself is a spatial metaphor, and any framework is likely to be projected in space, even confused or identified with its spatial projection. In Dante Eden is a long way up, on top of the mountain of purgatory; heaven is much further up, and hell is down, at the center of the earth. We may know that such conceptions as heaven and hell do not depend on spatial metaphors of up and down, but a cosmological poet, dealing with them as images, has to put them somewhere. To Dante it was simple enough to put them at the top and bottom of the natural order, because he knew of no alternative to the Ptolemaic picture of the world. To Milton, who did know of an alternative, the problem was more complex, and Milton's heaven and hell are outside the cosmos, in a kind of absolute up and down. After Milton comes Newton, and after Newton ups and downs become hopelessly confused.

What I see first of all in Romanticism is the effect of a profound change, not primarily in belief, but in the spatial projection of reality. This in turn leads to a different localizing of the various levels of that reality. Such a change in the localizing of images is bound to be accompanied by, or even cause, changes in belief and attitude, and changes of this latter sort are exhibited by the Romantic poets. But the change itself is not in belief or attitude, and may be found in, or at least affecting, poets of a great variety of beliefs.

In the earlier framework, the disorder of sin, death, and corruption was restricted to the sublunary world of four elements. Above the moon was all that was left of nature as God had originally planned it before the fall. The planets, with their angel-guided spheres, are images of a divinely sanctioned order of nature which is also the true home of man. Hence there was no poetic incongruity in Dante's locating his Paradiso in the planetary spheres, nor in Milton's associating the music of the spheres with the song of the angels in the *Nativity Ode,* nor in using the same word "heaven" for both the kingdom of God and the sky. A post-Newtonian poet has to think of gravitation and the solar system. Newton, Miss Nicolson has reminded us, demanded the muse, but the appropriate muse was Urania, and Urania had already been requested by Milton to descend to a safer position on earth for the second half of *Paradise Lost*.

Let us turn to Blake's poem *Europe,* engraved in 1794. *Europe* surveys the history of the Western world from the birth of Christ to the beginning of the French Revolution, and in its opening lines parodies the *Nativity Ode*. For Blake all the deities associated with the planets and the starry skies, of whom the chief is Enith-armon, the Queen of Heaven, are projections of a human will to tyranny, rationalized as eternal necessity and order. Christianity, according to this poem, had not abolished but confirmed the natural religion in the classical culture which had deified the star-gods. The doom of tyranny is sealed by the French Revolution, and the angel who blows the last trumpet as the sign of the final awakening of liberty is Isaac Newton. The frontispiece of *Europe* is the famous vision of the sky-god Urizen generally called the Ancient of Days, holding a compass in his left hand, and this picture is closely related to Blake's portrait of Newton, similarly preoccupied with a compass and oblivious of the heavens he is supposed to be studying.

Blake's view, in short, is that the universe of modern astronomy, as revealed in Newton, exhibits only a blind, mechanical, subhu-man order, not the personal presence of a deity. Newton himself tended to think of God still as "up there," even to the extent of suggesting that space was the divine sensorium; but *what* was up there, according to Blake, is only a set of interlocking geo-metrical diagrams, and God, Blake says, is not a mathematical diagram. Newtonism leads to what for Blake are intellectual errors, such as a sense of the superiority of abstractions to actual things and the notion that the real world is a measurable but invisible world of primary qualities. But Blake's main point is that admiring the mechanisms of the sky leads to establishing human life in mechanical patterns too. In other words, Blake's myth of Urizen is a fuller and more sophisticated version of the myth of Frankenstein.

Blake's evil, sinister, or merely complacent sky-gods, Urizen, Nobodaddy, Enitharmon, Satan, remind us of similar beings in other Romantics: Shelley's Jupiter, Byron's Arimanes, the Lord in the Prologue to *Faust*. They in their turn beget later Romantic gods and goddesses, such as Baudelaire's female "froide majesté," Hardy's Immanent Will, or the God of Housman's "The chestnut casts his flambeaux," who is a brute and blackguard because he is a sky-god in control of the weather, and sends his rain on the just and on the unjust. The association of sinister or unconscious mechanism with what we now call outer space is a commonplace of popular literature today which is a Romantic inheritance. Perhaps Orwell's *1984,* a vision of a mechanical tyranny informed by the shadow of a Big Brother who can never die, is the terminal point of a development of imagery that began with Blake's Ancient of Days. Not every poet, naturally, associates mechanism with the movements of the stars as Blake does, or sees it as a human imitation of the wrong kind of divine creativity. But the contrast between the mechanical and the organic is deeply rooted in Romantic thinking, and the tendency is to associate the mechanical with ordinary consciousness, as we see in the account of the associative fancy in Coleridge's *Biographia* or of discursive thought in Shelley's *Defence of Poetry.* This is in striking contrast to the Cartesian tradition, where the mechanical is of course associated with the subconscious. The mechanical being characteristic of ordinary experience, it is found particularly in the world "outside"; the superior or organic world is consequently "inside," and although it is still called superior or higher, the natural metaphorical direction of the inside world is downward, into the profounder depths of consciousness.

If a Romantic poet, therefore, wishes to write of God, he has more difficulty in finding a place to put him than Dante or even Milton had, and on the whole he prefers to do without a place, or finds "within" metaphors more reassuring than "up there" metaphors. When Wordsworth speaks, in *The Prelude* and elsewhere, of feeling the presence of deity through a sense of interpenetration of the human mind and natural powers, one feels that his huge and mighty forms, like the spirits of Yeats, have come to bring him the right metaphors for his poetry. In the second book of *The Excursion* we have a remarkable vision of what has been called the heavenly city of the eighteenth-century philosophers, cast in the form of an ascent up a mountain, where the city is seen at the top. The symbolism, I think, is modeled on the vision of Cleopolis in the first book of *The Faerie Queene,* and its technique is admirably controlled and precise. Yet surely this is not the real Wordsworth. The spirits have brought him the wrong metaphors; metaphors that Spenser used with full imaginative conviction, but which affect only the surface of Wordsworth's mind.

The second level of the older construct was the world of original human nature, now a lost paradise or golden age. It is conceived as a better and more appropriate home for man than his present environment, whether man can regain it or not. But in the older construct this world was ordinarily not thought of as human in origin or conception. Adam awoke in a garden not of his planting, in a fresh-air suburb of the City of God, and when the descendants of Cain began to build cities on earth, they were building to models already existing in both heaven and hell. In the Middle Ages and the Renaissance the agencies which helped to raise man from the physical to the human world were such things as the sacraments of religion, the moral law, and the habit of virtue, none of them strictly human inventions. These were the safe and unquestioned agencies, the genuinely educational media. Whether the human arts of poetry and painting and music were genuinely educational in this sense could be and was disputed or denied; and the poets themselves, when they wrote apologies for poetry, seldom claimed equality with religion or law, beyond pointing out that the earliest major poets were prophets and lawgivers.

For the modern mind there are two poles of mental activity. One may be described as sense, by which I mean the recognition of what is presented by experience: the empirical, observant habit of mind in which, among other things, the inductive sciences begin. In this attitude reality is, first of all, "out there," whatever happens to it afterwards. The other pole is the purely formalizing or constructive aspect of the mind, where reality is something brought into being by the act of construction. It is obvious that in pre-Romantic poetry there is a strong affinity with the attitude that we have called sense. The poet, in all ages and cultures, prefers images to abstractions, the sensational to the conceptual. But the pre-Romantic structure of imagery belonged to a nature

which was the work of God; the design in nature was, as Sir
Thomas Browne calls it, the art of God; nature is thus an objective structure or system for the poet to follow. The appropriate
metaphors of imitation are visual and physical ones, and the creative powers of the poet have models outside him.

It is generally recognized that Rousseau represents, and to some
extent made, a revolutionary change in the modern attitude. The
primary reason for his impact was, I think, not in his political
or educational views as such, but in his assumption that civilization was a purely human artifact, something that man had made,
could unmake, could subject to his own criticism, and was at all
times entirely responsible for. Above all, it was something for
which the only known model was in the human mind. This kind
of assumption is so penetrating that it affects those who detest
Rousseau, or have never heard of him, equally with the small
minority of his admirers. Also, it gets into the mind at once,
whereas the fading out of such counter assumptions as the literal
and historical nature of the Garden of Eden story is very gradual.
The effect of such an assumption is twofold. First, it puts the
arts in the center of civilization. The basis of civilization is now
the creative power of man; its model is the human vision revealed
in the arts. Second, this model, as well as the sources of creative
power, are now located in the mind's internal heaven, the external world being seen as a mirror reflecting and making visible
what is within. Thus the "outside" world, most of which is "up
there," yields importance and priority to the inner world, in fact
derives its poetic significance at least from it. "In looking at objects of Nature," says Coleridge in the Notebooks, "I seem rather
to be seeking, as it were *asking* for, a symbolical language for

something within me that already and forever exists, than observing anything new." This principle extends both to the immediate surrounding world which is the emblem of the music of humanity in Wordsworth and to the starry heavens on which Keats read "Huge cloudy symbols of a high romance."

Hence in Romantic poetry the emphasis is not on what we have called sense, but on the constructive power of the mind, where reality is brought into being by experience. There is a contrast in popular speech between the romantic and the realist, where the word "romantic" implies a sentimentalized or rose-colored view of reality. This vulgar sense of the word may throw some light on the intensity with which the Romantic poets sought to defy external reality by creating a uniformity of tone and mood. The establishing of this uniformity, and the careful excluding of anything that would dispel it, is one of the constant and typical features of the best Romantic poetry, though we may call it a dissociation of sensibility if we happen not to like it. Such a poetic technique is, psychologically, akin to magic, which also aims at bringing spiritual forces into reality through concentration on a certain type of experience. Such words as "charm" or "spell" suggest uniformity of mood as well as a magician's repertoire. Historically and generically, it is akin to romance, with its effort to maintain a self-consistent idealized world without the intrusions of realism or irony.

For these reasons Romanticism is difficult to adapt to the novel, which demands an empirical and observant attitude; its contribution to prose fiction is rather, appropriately enough, a form of romance. In the romance the characters tend to become psychological projections, and the setting a period in a past just remote enough to be re-created rather than empirically studied. We think of Scott as within the Romantic movement; Jane Austen as related to it chiefly by her parodies of the kind of sensibility that tries to live in a self-created world instead of adapting to the one that is there. Marianne in *Sense and Sensibility,* Catherine in *Northanger Abbey,* and of course everybody in *Love and Freindship,* are examples. Crabbe's naturalistic manifesto in the opening of *The Village* expresses an attitude which in itself is not far from Wordsworth's. But Crabbe is a metrical novelist in a way that Wordsworth is not. The soldier in *The Prelude* and the leech-gatherer in *Resolution and Independence* are purely romantic characters in the sense just given of psychological projections: that is, they become temporary or epiphanic myths. We should also notice that the internalizing of reality in Romanticism proper develops a contrast between it and a contemporary realism which descends from the pre-Romantic tradition but acquires a more purely empirical attitude to the external world.

The third level of the older construct was the physical world, theologically fallen, which man is born into but which is not the real world of human nature. Man's primary attitude to external physical nature is thus one of detachment. The kind of temptation represented by Spenser's Bower of Bliss or Milton's Comus is based on the false suggestion that physical nature, with its relatively innocent moral freedom, can be the model for human nature. The resemblances between the poetic techniques used in the Bower of Bliss episode and some of the techniques of the Romantics are superficial: Spenser, unlike the Romantics, is consciously producing a rhetorical set piece, designed to show that the Bower of Bliss is not natural but artificial in the modern

sense. Man for pre-Romantic poets is not a child of Nature in
the sense that he was originally a primitive. Milton's Adam becomes a noble savage immediately after his fall; but that is not
his original nature. In Romanticism the cult of the primitive is
a by-product of the internalizing of the creative impulse. The poet
has always been supposed to be imitating nature, but if the model
of his creative power is in his mind, the nature that he is to
imitate is now inside him, even if it is also outside.

The original form of human society also is hidden "within."
Keats refers to this hidden society when he says in a letter to
Reynolds: "Man should not dispute or assert but whisper results
to his neighbour . . . and Humanity . . . would become a grand
democracy of Forest Trees!" Coleridge refers to it in the *Biographia* when he says: "The medium, by which spirits understand each other, is not the surrounding air; but the *freedom*
which they possess in common." Whether the Romantic poet
is revolutionary or conservative depends on whether he regards
this original society as concealed by or as manifested in existing
society. If the former, he will think of true society as a primitive
structure of nature and reason, and will admire the popular,
simple, or even the barbaric more than the sophisticated. If the
latter, he will find his true inner society manifested by a sacramental church or by the instinctive manners of an aristocracy.
The search for a visible ideal society in history leads to a good
deal of admiration for the Middle Ages, which on the Continent
was sometimes regarded as the essential feature of Romanticism.
The affinity between the more extreme Romantic conservatism
and the subversive revolutionary movements of fascism and
nazism in our day has been often pointed out. The present sig-

nificance for us of this fact is that the notion of the inwardness of creative power is inherently revolutionary, just as the pre-Romantic construct was inherently conservative, even for poets as revolutionary as Milton. The self-identifying admiration which so many Romantics expressed for Napoleon has much to do with the association of natural force, creative power, and revolutionary outbreak. As Carlyle says, in an uncharacteristically cautious assessment of Napoleon: "What Napoleon *did* will in the long-run amount to what he did *justly;* what Nature with her laws will sanction."

Further, the Romantic poet is a part of a total process, engaged with and united to a creative power greater than his own because it includes his own. This greater creative power has a relation to him which we may call, adapting a term of Blake's, his vehicular form. The sense of identity with a larger power of creative energy meets us everywhere in Romantic culture, I think even in the crowded excited canvases of Delacroix and the tremendous will-to-power finales of Beethoven. The symbolism of it in literature has been too thoroughly studied in Professor Abrams's *The Mirror and the Lamp* and in Professor Wasserman's *The Subtler Language* for me to add more than a footnote or two at this point. Sometimes the greater power of this vehicular form is a rushing wind, as in Shelley's Ode and in the figure of the "correspondent breeze" studied by Professor Abrams. The image of the Aeolian harp, or lyre—Romantic poets are apt to be sketchy in their orchestration—belongs here. Sometimes it is a boat driven by a breeze or current, or by more efficient magical forces in the *Ancient Mariner*. This image occurs so often in Shelley that it has helped to suggest my title; the introduction to Wordsworth's *Peter Bell* has a flying boat closely associated with the moon. Those poems of Wordsworth in which we feel driven along by a propelling metrical energy, *Peter Bell, The Idiot Boy, The Waggoner,* and others, seem to me to be among Wordsworth's most central poems. Sometimes the vehicular form is a heightened state of consciousness in which we feel that we are greater than we know, or an intense feeling of communion, as in the sacramental corn-and-wine images of the great Keats odes.

The sense of unity with a greater power is surely one of the reasons why so much of the best Romantic poetry is mythopoeic. The myth is typically the story of the god, whose form and character are human but who is also a sun-god or tree-god or ocean-god. It identifies the human with the nonhuman world, an identification which is also one of the major functions of poetry itself. Coleridge makes it a part of the primary as well as the secondary imagination. "This I call *I*," he says in the Notebooks, "identifying the percipient and the perceived." The "Giant Forms" of Blake's prophecies are states of being and feeling in which we have our own being and feeling; the huge and mighty forms of Wordsworth's *Prelude* have similar affinities; even the dreams of De Quincey seem vehicular in the same sense. It is curious that there seems to be so little mythopoeic theory in Romantic poets, considering that the more expendable critics of the time complained as much about the obscurity of myth as their counterparts of today do now.

One striking feature of the Romantic poets is their resistance to fragmentation: their compulsion, almost, to express themselves in long continuous poems is quite as remarkable as their lyrical gifts. I have remarked elsewhere that the romance, in its most naive and primitive form, is an endless sequence of adventures, terminated only by the author's death or disgust. In Romanticism something of this inherently endless romance form recurs. *Childe Harold* and *Don Juan* are Byron to such an extent that the poems about them can be finished only by Byron's death or boredom with the *persona. The Prelude,* and still more the gigantic scheme of which it formed part, has a similar relation to Wordsworth, and something parallel is beginning to show its head at once in Keats's *Sleep and Poetry* and Shelley's *Queen Mab.* We touch here on the problem of the Romantic unfinished poem, which has been studied by Professor Bostetter. My present interest, however, is rather in the feature of unlimited continuity, which seems to me connected with the sense of vehicular energy, of being carried along by a greater force, the quality which outside literature, according to Keats, makes a man's life a continual allegory.

We have found, then, that the metaphorical structure of Romantic poetry tends to move inside and downward instead of outside and upward, hence the creative world is deep within, and so is heaven or the place of the presence of God. Blake's Orc and Shelley's Prometheus are Titans imprisoned underneath experience; the Gardens of Adonis are down in *Endymion,* whereas they are up in *The Faerie Queene* and *Comus;* in *Prometheus Unbound* everything that aids mankind comes from below, associated with volcanoes and fountains. In *The Revolt of*

Islam there is a curious collision with an older habit of metaphor
when Shelley speaks of

> A power, a thirst, a knowledge . . . below
> All thoughts, like light beyond the atmosphere.

The *Kubla Khan* geography of caves and underground streams
haunts all of Shelley's language about creative processes: in
Speculations on Metaphysics, for instance, he says: "But thought
can with difficulty visit the intricate and winding chambers
which it inhabits. It is like a river whose rapid and perpetual
stream flows outwards. . . . The caverns of the mind are obscure, and shadowy, or pervaded with a lustre, beautifully bright
indeed, but shining not beyond their portals."

In pre-Romantic poetry heaven is the order of grace, and grace
is normally thought of as descending from above into the soul.
In the Romantic construct there is a center where inward and
outward manifestations of a common motion and spirit are unified, where the ego is identified as itself because it is also identified
with something which is not itself. In Blake this world at the
deep center is Jerusalem, the City of God that mankind, or Albion,
has sought all through history without success because he has
been looking in the wrong direction, outside. Jerusalem is also
the garden of Eden where the Holy Word walked among the
ancient trees; Eden in the unfallen world would be the same
place as England's green and pleasant land where Christ also
walked; and England's green and pleasant land is also Atlantis,
the sunken island kingdom which we can rediscover by drain-
ing the "Sea of Time and Space" off the top of the mind. In

Prometheus Unbound Atlantis reappears when Prometheus is liberated, and the one great flash of vision which is all that is left to us of Wordsworth's *Recluse* uses the same imagery.

> Paradise, and groves
> Elysian, Fortunate Fields—like those of old
> Sought in the Atlantic Main—why should they be
> A history only of departed things,
> Or a mere fiction of what never was? . . .
> —I, long before the blissful hour arrives,
> Would chant, in lonely peace, the spousal verse
> Of this great consummation.

The Atlantis theme is in many other Romantic myths: in the Glaucus episode of *Endymion* and in De Quincey's *Savannah-la-Mar,* which speaks of "human life still subsisting in submarine asylums sacred from the storms that torment our upper air." The theme of land reclaimed from the ocean plays also a somewhat curious role in Goethe's *Faust.* We find the same imagery in later writers who continue the Romantic tradition, such as D. H. Lawrence in the "Song of a Man Who Has Come Through":

> If only I am keen and hard like the sheer tip of a wedge
> Driven by invisible blows,
> The rock will split, we shall come at the wonder, we shall find
> the Hesperides.

In *The Pilgrim's Progress* Ignorance is sent to hell from the very gates of heaven. The inference seems to be that only Ignorance knows the precise location of both kingdoms. For knowledge, and still more for imagination, the journey within to the happy island garden or the city of light is a perilous quest, equally likely to terminate in the blasted ruin of Byron's *Darkness* or Beddoes's *Subterranean City*. In many Romantic poems, including Keats's nightingale ode, it is suggested that the final identification of and with reality may be or at least include death. The suggestion that death may lead to the highest knowledge, dropped by Lucifer in Byron's *Cain,* haunts Shelley continually. A famous passage in *Prometheus Unbound* associates the worlds of creation and death in the same inner area, where Zoroaster meets his image in a garden. Just as the sun is the means but not a tolerable object of sight, so the attempt to turn around and see the source of one's vision may be destructive, as the Lady of Shalott found when she turned away from the mirror. Thus the world of the deep interior in Romantic poetry is morally ambivalent, retaining some of the demonic qualities that the corresponding pre-Romantic lowest level had.

This sense that the source of genius is beyond good and evil, that the possession of genius may be a curse, that the only real knowledge given to Adam in Paradise, however disastrous, came to him from the devil—all this is part of the contribution of Byron to modern sensibility, and part of the irrevocable change that he made in it. Of his Lara Byron says:

> He stood a stranger in this breathing world,
> An erring spirit from another hurl'd;
> A thing of dark imaginings, that shaped
> By choice the perils he by chance escaped;
> But 'scaped in vain, for in their memory yet

His mind would half exult and half regret . . .
But haughty still and loth himself to blame,
He call'd on Nature's self to share the shame,
And charged all faults upon the fleshly form
She gave to clog the soul, and feast the worm;
Till he at last confounded good and ill,
And half mistook for fate the acts of will.

It would be wrong to regard this as Byronic hokum, for the wording is very precise. Lara looks demonic to a nervous and conforming society, as the dragon does to the tame villatic fowl in Milton. But there is a genuinely demonic quality in him which arises from his being nearer than other men to the unity of subjective and objective worlds. To be in such a place might make a poet more creative; it makes other types of superior beings, including Lara, more destructive.

We said earlier that a Romantic poet's political views would depend partly on whether he saw his inner society as concealed by or as manifested in actual society. A Romantic poet's moral attitude depends on a similar ambivalence in the conception of nature. Nature to Wordsworth is a mother-goddess who teaches the soul serenity and joy, and never betrays the heart that loves her; to the Marquis de Sade nature is the source of all the perverse pleasures that an earlier age had classified as "unnatural." For Wordsworth the reality of Nature is manifested by its reflection of moral values; for De Sade the reality is concealed by that reflection. It is this ambivalent sense (for it is ambivalent, and not simply ambiguous) of appearance as at the same time revealing and concealing reality, as clothes simultaneously reveal

and conceal the naked body, that makes *Sartor Resartus* so central
a document of the Romantic movement. We spoke of Wordsworth's Nature as a mother-goddess, and her psychological descent
from mother-figures is clearly traced in *The Prelude.* The corn-
goddess in Keats's *To Autumn,* the parallel figure identified with
Ruth in the *Ode to a Nightingale,* the still unravished bride of
the Grecian urn, Psyche, even the veiled Melancholy, are all em-
blems of a revealed Nature. Elusive nymphs or teasing and
mocking female figures who refuse to take definite form, like
the figure in *Alastor* or Blake's "female will" types; terrible and
sinister white goddesses like La Belle Dame sans Merci, or females
associated with something forbidden or demonic, like the sister-
lovers of Byron and Shelley, belong to the concealed aspect.

For Wordsworth, who still has a good deal of the pre-Romantic
sense of nature as an objective order, nature is a landscape nature,
and from it, as in Baudelaire's *Correspondances,* mysterious oracles
seep into the mind through eye or ear, even a bird with so pre-
dictable a song as the cuckoo being an oracular wandering voice.
This landscape is a veil dropped over the naked nature of scream-
ing rabbits and gasping stags, the nature red in tooth and claw
which haunted a later generation. Even the episode of the dog
and the hedgehog in *The Prelude* is told from the point of view
of the dog and not of the hedgehog. But the more pessimistic,
and perhaps more realistic, conception of nature in which it can
be a source of evil or suffering as well as good is the one that
gains ascendancy in the later period of Romanticism, and its
later period extends to our own day.

The major constructs which our own culture has inherited
from its Romantic ancestry are also of the "drunken boat" shape,

but represent a later and a different conception of it from the "vehicular form" described above. Here the boat is usually in the position of Noah's ark, a fragile container of sensitive and imaginative values threatened by a chaotic and unconscious power below it. In Schopenhauer, the world as idea rides precariously on top of a "world as will" which engulfs practically the whole of existence in its moral indifference. In Darwin, who readily combines with Schopenhauer, as the later work of Hardy illustrates, consciousness and morality are accidental sports from a ruthlessly competitive evolutionary force. In Freud, who has noted the resemblance of his mythical structure to Schopenhauer's, the conscious ego struggles to keep afloat on a sea of libidinous impulse. In Kierkegaard, all the "higher" impulses of fallen man pitch and roll on the surface of a huge and shapeless "dread." In some versions of this construct the antithesis of the symbol of consciousness and the destructive element in which it is immersed can be overcome or transcended: there is an Atlantis under the sea which becomes an Ararat for the beleaguered boat to rest on.

I give an example from Auden, partly because he is prominently featured in this session of the Institute, and partly to show that the Romantic structures of symbolism are still ours. In Freud, when the conscious mind feels threatened by the subconscious, it tries to repress it, and so develops a neurosis In Marx, the liberal elements in an ascendant class, when they feel threatened by a revolutionary situation, develop a police state. In both cases the effort is to intensify the antithesis between the two, but this effort is mistaken, and when the barriers are broken down we reach the balanced mind and the classless society respectively.

For the Time Being develops a religious construct out of Kierkegaard on the analogy of those of Marx and Freud. The liberal
or rational elements represented by Herod feel threatened by
the revival of superstition in the Incarnation, and try to repress
it. Their failure means that the effort to come to terms with a
nature outside the mind, the primary effort of reason, has to be
abandoned, and this enables the Paradise or divine presence which
is locked up inside the human mind to manifest itself after the
reason has searched the whole of objective nature in vain to find
it. The attitude is that of a relatively orthodox Christianity; the
imagery and the structure of symbolism is that of *Prometheus
Unbound* and *The Marriage of Heaven and Hell.*

In Romanticism proper a prominent place in sense experience
is given to the ear, an excellent receiver of oracles but poor in
locating things accurately in space. This latter power, which is
primarily visual, is associated with the fancy in Wordsworth's
1815 preface, and given the subordinate position appropriate to
fancy. In later poetry, beginning with *symbolisme* in France,
when there is a good deal of reaction against earlier Romanticism, more emphasis is thrown on vision. In Rimbaud, though
his *Bateau Ivre* has given me my title, the poet is to *se faire
voyant,* the *illuminations* are thought of pictorially; even the
vowels must be visually colored. Such an emphasis has nothing
to do with the pre-Romantic sense of an objective structure in
nature: on the contrary, the purpose of it is to intensify the
Romantic sense of oracular significance into a kind of autohypnosis. (The association of autohypnosis and the visual sense
is discussed in Professor Marshall McLuhan's new book, *The
Gutenberg Galaxy.*) Such an emphasis leads to a technique of

fragmentation. Poe's attack on the long poem is not a Romantic but an anti-Romantic manifesto, as the direction of its influence indicates. The tradition of *symbolisme* is present in imagism, where the primacy of visual values is so strongly stated in theory and so cheerfully ignored in practice, in Pound's emphasis on the spatial juxtaposing of metaphor, in Eliot's insistence on the superiority of poets who present the "clear visual images" of Dante. T. E. Hulme's attack on the Romantic tradition is consistent in preferring fancy to imagination and in stressing the objectivity of the nature to be imitated; less so in his primitivism and his use of Bergson. The technique of fragmentation is perhaps intended to reach its limit in Pound's publication of the complete poetical works of Hulme on a single page.

As I have tried to indicate by my reference to Auden, what this anti-Romantic movement did not do was to create a third framework of imagery. Nor did it return to the older construct, though Eliot, by sticking closely to Dante and by deprecating the importance of the prophetic element in art, gives some illusion of doing so. The charge of subjectivity, brought against the Romantics by Arnold and often repeated later, assumes that objectivity is a higher attribute of poetry, but this is itself a Romantic conception, and came into English criticism with Coleridge. Anti-Romanticism, in short, had no resources for becoming anything more than a post-Romantic movement. The first phase of the "reconsideration" of Romanticism discussed by this group is to understand its continuity with modern literature, and this phase is now well developed in the work of Professor Kermode and others. All we need do to complete it is to examine Romanticism by its own standards and canons. We should not look

for precision where vagueness is wanted; not extol the virtues
of constipation when the Romantics were exuberant; not insist
on visual values when the poet listens darkling to a nightingale.
Then, perhaps, we may see in Romanticism also the quality that
Melville found in Greek architecture:

Not innovating wilfulness,
But reverence for the Archetype.

M. H. Abrams

ENGLISH ROMANTICISM: THE SPIRIT OF THE AGE

MY TITLE echoes that of William Hazlitt's remarkable book of 1825, which set out to represent what we now call the climate of opinion among the leading men of his time. In his abrupt way Hazlitt did not stay to theorize, plunging into the middle of things with a sketch of Jeremy Bentham. But from these essays emerges plainly his view that the crucial occurrence for his generation had been the French Revolution. In that event and its repercussions, political, intellectual, and imaginative, and in the resulting waves of hope and gloom, revolutionary loyalty and recreancy, he saw both the promise and the failures of his violent and contradictory era.

The span covered by the active life of Hazlitt's subjects—approximately the early 1790s to 1825—coincides with what literary historians now call the Romantic period; and it is Hazlitt's contention that the characteristic poetry of the age took its shape from the form and pressure of revolution and reaction. The whole "Lake school of poetry," he had said seven years earlier, "had its origin in the French revolution, or rather in those sentiments and opinions which produced that revolution." [1] Hazlitt's main

[1] *Lectures on the English Poets* (1818), in *The Complete Works of William Hazlitt,* ed. P. P. Howe (21 vols.; London, 1930–34), V, 161.

exhibit is Wordsworth (the "head" of the school), whose "genius,"
he declares, "is a pure emanation of the Spirit of the Age." The
poetry of Wordsworth in the period of *Lyrical Ballads* was "one
of the innovations of the time."

> It partakes of, and is carried along with, the revolutionary
> movement of our age: the political changes of the day were
> the model on which he formed and conducted his poetical
> experiments. His Muse (it cannot be denied, and without this
> we cannot explain its character at all) is a levelling one.[2]

Neither the concept that the age had an identifying "spirit,"
nor that this spirit was one of revolutionary change, was unique
with Hazlitt. Just after the revolution of July, 1830, John Stuart
Mill wrote a series of essays on *The Spirit of the Age* in which
he said that the phrase, denoting "the dominant idea" of the
times, went back only some fifty years, and resulted from the
all but universal conviction "that the times are pregnant with
change"—a condition "of which the first overt manifestation
was the breaking out of the French Revolution." [3] Shelley, in
A Philosophical View of Reform (1819), after reviewing the
European outbreaks of liberty against tyranny which culminated
in the American and French revolutions, asserted that the related
crisis of change in England had been accompanied by a literary

[2] *The Spirit of the Age, ibid.,* XI, 86–87.

[3] John Stuart Mill, *The Spirit of the Age,* ed. Frederick A. von Hayek
(Chicago, 1942), pp. 1–2, 67. In 1812 Thomas Belsham spoke of "the
spirit of the times," the "mania of the French Revolution," which "pervaded all ranks of society" (*Memoirs of the Late Reverend Theophilus
Lindsey* [2d ed.; London, 1820], p. 216). See also "Letter on the Spirit
of the Age," *Blackwood's Magazine,* XXVIII (Dec., 1830), 900–920.

renascence, in which the poets displayed "a comprehensive and all-penetrating spirit" that was "less their own spirit than the spirit of their age."[4] Conservative critics, like the radical Shelley, recognized the fact of a great new poetry and associated its genesis with political events. "The revolution in our literature," Francis Jeffrey claimed in 1816, had as one of its primary causes "the agitations of the French revolution, and the discussions as well as the hopes and terrors to which it gave occasion."[5] And De Quincey said (1839) that the almost "miraculous" effect of the "great moral tempest" of the Revolution was evident "in all lands . . . and at the same time." "In Germany or England alike, the poetry was so entirely regenerated, thrown into moulds of thought and of feeling so new, that the poets everywhere felt themselves . . . entering upon the dignity and the sincere thinking of mature manhood."[6]

It seems to me that Hazlitt and his contemporary viewers of the literary scene were, in their general claim, manifestly right: the Romantic period was eminently an age obsessed with the fact of violent and inclusive change, and Romantic poetry

[4] *Shelley's Prose*, ed. David Lee Clark (Albuquerque, 1954), pp. 239–40; the passage was later used, almost verbatim, as the conclusion of *A Defence of Poetry*. See also the Preface to *Prometheus Unbound, ibid.*, pp. 327–28, and the letter to C. and J. Ollier, Oct. 15, 1819. Shelley called the French Revolution "the master theme of the epoch in which we live" (*Lord Byron's Correspondence*, ed. John Murray [2 vols.; London, 1922], II, 15).

[5] Review of Walter Scott's edition of *The Works of Jonathan Swift*, in *Contributions to the Edinburgh Review* (4 vols.; London, 1844), I, 158–67.

[6] "William Wordsworth," in *The Collected Writings of Thomas De Quincey*, ed. David Masson (14 vols.; Edinburgh, 1889–90), II, 273–74.

cannot be understood, historically, without awareness of the degree to which this preoccupation affected its substance and form. The phenomenon is too obvious to have escaped notice, in monographs devoted to the French Revolution and the English poets, singly and collectively. But when critics and historians turn to the general task of defining the distinctive qualities of "Romanticism," or of the English Romantic movement, they usually ignore its relations to the revolutionary climate of the time. For example, in an anthology of "the 'classic' statements" on Romanticism, especially in England, which came out in 1962, the few essays which give more than passing mention to the French Revolution do so to reduce the particularity of Romantic poems mainly to a distant reflection of an underlying economic reality, and to an unconscious rationalization of the bourgeois illusion of "freedom." [7]

It may be useful, then, to have a new look at the obvious as it appeared, not to post-Marxist historians, but to intelligent observers at the time. I shall try to indicate briefly some of the ways in which the political, intellectual, and emotional circumstances of a period of revolutionary upheaval affected the scope, subject-matter, themes, values, and even language of a number of Romantic poems. I hope to avoid easy and empty generalizations about the *Zeitgeist,* and I do not propose the electrifying proposition that "le romantisme, c'est la révolution." Romanticism is no one thing. It is many very individual poets, who wrote poems manifesting a greater diversity of qualities, it seems

[7] *Romanticism: Points of View,* ed. Robert F. Gleckner and Gerald E. Enscoe (Englewood Cliffs, N.J., 1962).

to me, than those of any preceding age. But some prominent qualities a number of these poems share, and certain of these shared qualities form a distinctive complex which may, with a high degree of probability, be related to the events and ideas of the cataclysmic coming-into-being of the world to which we are by now becoming fairly accustomed.

I. THE SPIRIT OF THE 1790S

By force of chronological habit we think of English Romanticism as a nineteenth-century phenomenon, overlooking how many of its distinctive features had been established by the end of the century before. The last decade of the eighteenth century included the complete cycle of the Revolution in France, from what De Quincey called its "gorgeous festival era" [8] to the *coup d'état* of November 10, 1799, when to all but a few stubborn sympathizers it seemed betrayed from without and within, and the portent of Napoleon loomed over Europe. That same decade was the period in which the poets of the first Romantic generation reached their literary maturity and had either completed, or laid out and begun, the greater number of what we now account their major achievements. By the end of the decade Blake was well along with *The Four Zoas;* only *Milton* and *Jerusalem* belong to the nineteenth century. By the end of the year 1800 Wordsworth had already announced the over-all design and begun writing the two great undertakings of his poetic career; that is, he had finished most of the first two books and a number of scattered later passages of *The Prelude,* and of *The Recluse*

[8] "William Wordsworth," *Collected Writings,* II, 274.

he had written "Home at Grasmere" (which included the extraordinary section he later reprinted as the "Prospectus of the design and scope of the whole poem") as well as the first book of *The Excursion.* Coleridge wrote in the 1790s seven-tenths of all the nondramatic material in his collected poems.

"Few persons but those who have lived in it," Southey reminisced in his Tory middle age, "can conceive or comprehend what the memory of the French Revolution was, nor what a visionary world seemed to open upon those who were just entering it. Old things seemed passing away, and nothing was dreamt of but the regeneration of the human race." [9] The early years of the Revolution, a modern commentator has remarked, were "perhaps the happiest in the memory of civilized man," [10] and his estimate is justified by the ecstasy described by Wordsworth in *The Prelude*—"bliss was it in that dawn to be alive"—and expressed by many observers of France in its glad dawn. Samuel Romilly exclaimed in May, 1792: "It is the most glorious event, and the happiest for mankind, that has ever taken place since human affairs have been recorded." Charles James Fox was less restrained in his evaluation: "How much the greatest event it is that ever happened in the world! and how much the best!" [11] A generation earlier Dr. Johnson had written a con-

[9] *The Correspondence of Robert Southey with Caroline Bowles,* ed. Edward Dowden (Dublin, 1881), p. 52.

[10] M. Ray Adams, *Studies in the Literary Backgrounds of English Radicalism* (Lancaster, Pa., 1947), p. 7.

[11] Romilly in Alfred Cobban, ed., *The Debate on the French Revolution, 1789–1800* (London, 1950), p. 354; Fox as cited by Edward Dowden, *The French Revolution and English Literature* (New York, 1897), p. 9. "Era of happiness in the history of the world!" John Thelwall described the

cluding passage for Goldsmith's *The Traveller* which summed
up prevailing opinion:

> How small, of all that human hearts endure,
> That part which laws or kings can cause or cure!
> Still to ourselves in every place consigned,
> Our own felicity we make or find.

But now it seemed to many social philosophers that the revolution against the king and the old laws would cure everything
and establish felicity for everyone, everywhere. In 1791 Volney
took time out from his revolutionary activities to publish *Les
ruines, ou méditations sur les révolutions des empires,* in which
a supervisory Genius unveils to him the vision of the past, the
present, and then the "New Age," which had in fact already
begun in the American Revolution and was approaching its
realization in France. "Now," cries the author, "may I live! for
after this there is nothing which I am not daring enough to
hope." [12] Condorcet wrote his *Outline of the Progress of the
Human Spirit* as a doomed man hiding from the police of the
Reign of Terror, to vindicate his unshaken faith that the Revolution was a breakthrough in man's progress; he ends with the
vision of mankind's imminent perfection both in his social condition and in his intellectual and moral powers.[13] The equivalent
book in England was Godwin's *Political Justice,* written under

---

Revolution; "Dawn of a real golden age" (Charles Cestre, *John Thelwall*
[London, 1906], p. 171).

[12] C. F. C. de Volney, *The Ruins* (5th ed.; London, 1807), pp. 92, 98–
113.

[13] Marquis de Condorcet, *Outlines of an Historical View of the Progress
of the Human Mind* (London, 1795), pp. 261–62, 370–72.

impetus of the Revolution in 1791–93, which has its similar anticipation of mankind morally transformed, living in a state of total economic and political equality.[14]

The intoxicating sense that now everything was possible was not confined to systematic philosophers. In 1793, Hazlitt said, schemes for a new society "of virtue and happiness" had been published "in plays, poems, songs, and romances—made their way to the bar, crept into the church . . . got into the hearts of poets and the brains of metaphysicians . . . and turned the heads of almost the whole kingdom."[15] Anyone who has looked into the poems, the sermons, the novels, and the plays of the early 1790s will know that this is not a gross exaggeration. Man regenerate in a world made new; this was the theme of a multitude of writers notable, forgotten, or anonymous. In the Prologue to his highly successful play, *The Road to Ruin* (1792), Thomas Holcroft took the occasion to predict that the Revolution in France had set the torrent of freedom spreading,

To ease, happiness, art, science, wit, and genius to give birth;
Ay, to fertilize a world, and renovate old earth![16]

"Renovate old earth," "the regeneration of the human race"— the phrases reflect their origin, and indicate a characteristic difference between French and English radicalism. Most French philosophers of perfectibility (and Godwin, their representative

[14] William Godwin, *Enquiry Concerning Political Justice,* ed. F. E. L. Priestley (3 vols.; Toronto, 1946); see, e.g., II, 463–64, 528–29; III, 180–81.

[15] *Complete Works,* VII, 99. Some of this minor revolutionary literature is reviewed in M. Ray Adams, *Literary Backgrounds of English Radicalism,* and Allene Gregory, *The French Revolution and the English Novel* (New York, 1915).

[16] *The Road to Ruin* (1st ed.; London, 1792).

in England) were anticlerical skeptics or downright atheists, who claimed that they based their predictions on an inductive science of history and a Lockian science of man. The chief strength and momentum of English radicalism, on the other hand, came from the religious Nonconformists who, as true heirs of their embattled ancestors in the English Civil War, looked upon contemporary politics through the perspective of biblical prophecy. In a sermon on the French Revolution preached in 1791 the Reverend Mark Wilks proclaimed: "Jesus Christ was a Revolutionist; and the Revolution he came to effect was foretold in these words, 'He hath sent me to proclaim liberty to the captives.'"[17] The Unitarians—influential beyond their numbers because they included so large a proportion of scientists, literary men, and powerful pulpit orators—were especially given to projecting on the empirical science of human progress the pattern and detail of biblical prophecies, Messianic, millennial, and apocalyptic. "Hey for the New Jerusalem! The millennium!" Thomas Holcroft cried out, in the intoxication of first reading Paine's *The Rights of Man* (1791);[18] what this notorious atheist uttered lightly was the fervent but considered opinion of a number of his pious contemporaries. Richard Price, in 1785, had viewed the American Revolution as the most important step, next to the introduction of Christianity itself, in the fulfillment of the "old prophecies" of an empire of reason, virtue, and peace, when the

[17] *The Origin and Stability of the French Revolution: A Sermon Preached at St. Paul's Chapel, Norwich, July 14, 1791*, p. 5; quoted by Mark Schorer, *William Blake: The Politics of Vision* (New York, 1946), p. 205. For apocalyptic thinking among the Illuminists in France, see A. Viatte, *Les sources occultes du Romantisme* (2 vols.; Paris, 1928), chap. vi.

[18] C. Kegan Paul, *William Godwin: His Friends and Contemporaries* (2 vols.; London, 1876), I, 69.

wolf will "dwell with the lamb and the leopard with the kid."
"May we not see there the dawning of brighter days on earth,
and a new creation rising?" In the sermon of 1789 which evoked
the hurricane of Burke's *Reflections on the French Revolution,*
he sees that event capped by one even greater and more immediately promising: "I am thankful that I have lived to [see]
it: and I could almost say, *Lord, now lettest thou thy servant
depart in peace, for mine eyes have seen thy salvation."* [19] By 1793
the increasingly violent course of the Revolution inspired the
prophets to turn from Isaiah's relatively mild prelude to the
peaceable kingdom and "the new heavens and the new earth"
to the classic text of apocalyptic violence, the Book of Revelation. In February of that year Elhanan Winchester's *The Three
Woe Trumpets* interpreted the Revolution in France as the
precise fulfillment of those prophecies, with the seventh trumpet
just about to sound (Rev. 11) to bring on the final cataclysm and
announce the Second Advent of Christ, in a Kingdom which
should be "the greatest blessing to mankind that ever they enjoyed, or even found an idea of." [20] In 1791 Joseph Priestley,

[19] Richard Price, *Observations on the Importance of the American
Revolution* (London, 1785), pp. 6–7, 21; *A Discourse on the Love of Our
Country* (Nov. 4, 1789), in S. MacCoby, ed., *The English Radical Tradition, 1763–1914* (London, 1952), p. 54. The dissenter Nash wrote in reply
to Burke's *Reflections:* "As I am a believer in Revelation, I, of course,
live in the hope of better things; a millennium . . . a new heaven and a
new earth in which dwelleth righteousness . . . a state of equal liberty
and equal justice for all men." (*A Letter to the Right Hon. Edmund
Burke from a Dissenting Country Attorney* [Birmingham, 1790]. Quoted
by Anthony Lincoln, *Some Political and Social Ideas of English Dissent,
1763–1800* [Cambridge, 1938], p. 3.)
[20] Elhanan Winchester, *The Three Woe Trumpets* (1st American ed.;

scientist, radical philosopher, and a founder of the Unitarian
Society, had written his *Letters* in reply to Burke's *Reflections,*
in which he pronounced the American and French revolutions
to be the inauguration of the state of universal happiness and
peace "distinctly and repeatedly foretold in many prophecies, delivered more than two thousand years ago." Three years later
he expanded his views in *The Present State of Europe Compared
with Antient Prophecies.* Combining philosophical empiricism
with biblical fundamentalism, he related the convulsions of the
time to the Messianic prophecies in Isaiah and Daniel, the apocalyptic passages in various books of the New Testament, and
especially to the Book of Revelation, as a ground for confronting
"the great scene, that seems now to be opening upon us . . . with
tranquillity, and even with satisfaction," in the persuasion that
its "termination will be glorious and happy," in the advent of
"the millennium, or the future peaceable and happy state of the
world."[21] Wordsworth's Solitary, in *The Excursion,* no doubt
reflects an aspect of Wordsworth's own temperament, but the
chief model for his earlier career was Joseph Fawcett, famous
Unitarian preacher at the Old Jewry, and a poet as well. In
Wordsworth's rendering, we find him, in both song and sermon,

---

Boston, 1794), pp. 37–38, 71. Winchester also published in 1793 *The
Process and Empire of Christ: An Heroic Poem* in blank verse, in which
Books VIII to XII deal with the Second Advent, the Millennium, and the
apocalyptic "New Creation; or, The Renovation of the Heavens and Earth
after the Conflagration."

[21] *Letters to the Right Honourable Edmund Burke* (2d ed.; Birming-
ham, 1791), pp. 143–50; *The Present State of Europe Compared with
Antient Prophecies* (4th ed.; London, 1794), pp. 18 ff., 30–32. See also
Priestley's *Sermon Preached in Hackney, Apr. 19, 1793,* and *Observations
on the Increase of Infidelity* (1796).

projecting a dazzling vision of the French Revolution which fuses classical myth with Christian prophecy:

> I beheld
> Glory—beyond all glory ever seen,
> Confusion infinite of heaven and earth,
> Dazzling the soul. Meanwhile, prophetic harps
> In every grove were ringing, "War shall cease."
> . . . I sang Saturnian rule
> Returned,—a progeny of golden years
> Permitted to descend and bless mankind.
> —With promises the Hebrew Scriptures teem.
> . . . the glowing phrase
> Of ancient inspiration serving me,
> I promised also,—with undaunted trust
> Foretold, and added prayer to prophecy.[22]

The formative age of Romantic poetry was clearly one of apocalyptic expectations, or at least apocalyptic imaginings, which endowed the promise of France with the form and impetus of one of the deepest rooted and most compelling myths in the culture of Christian Europe.

II. THE VOICE OF THE BARD

In a verse-letter of 1800 Blake identified the crucial influences in his spiritual history as a series beginning with Milton and the Old Testament prophets and ending with the American War

[22] *The Excursion*, III, 716–65; also II, 210–23. On the relation of the Solitary to Joseph Fawcett see M. Ray Adams, *Literary Backgrounds of English Radicalism*, Chap. VII.

and the French Revolution.[23] Since Blake is the only major Romantic old enough to have published poems before the Revolution, his writings provide a convenient indication of the effects of that event and of the intellectual and emotional atmosphere that it generated.

As Northrop Frye has said in his fine book on Blake, his *Poetical Sketches* of 1783 associate him with Collins, Gray, the Wartons, and other writers of what Frye later called "The Age of Sensibility." [24] As early as the 1740s this school had mounted a literary revolution against the acknowledged tradition of Waller-Denham-Pope—a tradition of civilized and urbane verse, controlled by "good sense and judgment," addressed to a closely integrated upper class, in which the triumphs, as Joseph Warton pointed out, were mainly in "the didactic, moral, and satiric kind." [25] Against this tradition, the new poets raised the claim of a more daring, "sublime," and "primitive" poetry, represented in England by Spenser, Shakespeare, Milton, who exhibit the supreme virtues of spontaneity, invention, and an "enthusiastic" and "creative" imagination—by which was signified a poetry of inspired vision, related to divinity, and populated by allegorical and supernatural characters such as do not exist "in nature." [26]

[23] *The Complete Writings of William Blake,* ed. Geoffrey Keynes (London, 1957), p. 799.

[24] *Fearful Symmetry* (Princeton, 1947), pp. 167 ff.; "Towards Defining an Age of Sensibility," in *Eighteenth-Century English Literature: Modern Essays in Criticism,* ed. James L. Clifford (New York, 1959), pp. 311–18.

[25] *An Essay on the Genius and Writings of Pope,* II (London, 1782), 477.

[26] See M. H. Abrams, *The Mirror and the Lamp* (New York, 1953), pp. 274–76 and notes.

Prominent in this literature of revolt, however, was a timidity, a sense of frustration very different from the assurance of power and of an accomplished and continuing literary renascence expressed by a number of their Romantic successors: Coleridge's unhesitating judgment that Wordsworth's genius measured up to Milton's, and Wordsworth's solemn concurrence in this judgment; Leigh Hunt's opinion that, for all his errors, Wordsworth is "at the head of a new and great age of poetry"; Keats's conviction that "Great spirits now on earth are sojourning"; Shelley's confidence that "the literature of England . . . has arisen, as it were, from a new birth." [27] The poets of sensibility, on the contrary, had felt that they and all future writers were fated to be epigones of a tradition of unrecapturable magnificence. So Collins said in his "Ode on the Poetical Character" as, retreating from "Waller's myrtle shades," he tremblingly pursued Milton's "guiding steps"; "In Vain—

Heaven and Fancy, kindred powers,
Have now o'erturned the inspiring bowers,
Or curtained close such scene from every future view.

And Gray:

But not to one in this benighted age
    Is that diviner inspiration given,
That burns in Shakespeare's or in Milton's page,
    The pomp and prodigality of Heaven.

[27] Leigh Hunt, *The Feast of the Poets* (London, 1814), p. 90; Keats, sonnet, "Great Spirits Now on Earth"; *Shelley's Prose,* pp. 239–40.

So, in 1783, Blake complained to the Muses:

> How have you left the antient love
> That bards of old enjoy'd in you!

Besides *Poetical Sketches,* Blake's main achievements before the French Revolution were *Songs of Innocence* and *The Book of Thel,* which represent dwellers in an Eden trembling on the verge of experience. Suddenly in 1790 came *The Marriage of Heaven and Hell,* boisterously promulgating "Energy" in opposition to all inherited limits on human possibilities; to point the contemporary relevance, Blake appended a "Song of Liberty," which represents Energy as a revolutionary "son of fire," moving from America to France and crying the advent of an Isaian millennium:

EMPIRE IS NO MORE! AND NOW THE LION AND WOLF SHALL CEASE.

In 1791 appeared Blake's *The French Revolution,* in the form of a Miltonic epic. Of the seven books announced, only the first is extant, but this is enough to demonstrate that Blake, like Priestley and other religious radicals of the day, envisioned the Revolution as the portent of apocalypse. After five thousand years "the ancient dawn calls us/ To awake," the Abbé de Sieyès pleads for a peace, freedom, and equality which will effect a regained Eden —"the happy earth sing in its course,/ The mild peaceable nations be opened to heav'n, and men walk with their fathers in bliss"; when his plea is ignored, there are rumblings of a gathering Armageddon, and the book ends with the portent of a first resurrection: "And the bottoms of the world were open'd, and the graves of arch-angels unseal'd."

The "Introduction" to *Songs of Experience* (1794) calls on us to

attend the voice which will sing all Blake's poems from now on:
"Hear the voice of the Bard!/ Who Present, Past, & Future, sees,"
who calls to the lapsèd Soul and enjoins the earth to cease her cycle
and turn to the eternal day. This voice is that of the poet-prophets
of the Old and New Testaments, now descending on Blake from
its specifically British embodiment in that "bard of old," John
Milton. In his "minor prophecies," ending in 1795, Blake develops,
out of the heroic-scaled but still historical agents of his *French
Revolution,* the Giant Forms of his later mythical system. The
Bard becomes Los, the "Eternal Prophet" and father of "red Orc,"
who is the spirit of Energy bursting out in total spiritual, physical,
and political revolution; the argument of the song sung by Los,
however, remains that announced in *The French Revolution.* As
David Erdman has said, *Europe: A Prophecy* (1794) was written
at about the time Blake was illustrating Milton's "On the Morning of Christ's Nativity," and reinterprets that poem for his own
times.[28] Orc, here identified with Christ the revolutionary, comes
with the blare of the apocalyptic trumpet to vex nature out of her
sleep of 1,800 years, in a cataclysmic Second Coming in "the vine-
yards of Red France" which, however, heralds the day when both
the earth and its inhabitants will be resurrected in a joyous burst
of unbounded and lustful energy.[29]

By the year 1797 Blake launched out into the "strong heroic
Verse" of *Vala, or The Four Zoas,* the first of his three full-scale
epics, which recounts the total history of "The Universal Man"

[28] *Blake, Prophet Against Empire* (Princeton, 1954), pp. 246 ff.; and see
Frye, *Fearful Symmetry,* p. 262.

[29] *Europe: A Prophecy,* Plates 9, 12–15. See also *America: A Prophecy*
(1793), Plates 6, 8, 16; *The Song of Los* (1795), Plates 3, 7.

from the beginning, through "His fall into Division," to a future that explodes into the most spectacular and sustained apocalyptic set-piece since the Book of Revelation; in this holocaust "the evil is all consum'd" and "all things are chang'd, even as in ancient times." [30]

III. ROMANTIC ORACLES

No amount of historical explanation can make Blake out to be other than a phoenix among poets; but if we put his work into its historical and intellectual context, and alongside that of his poetic contemporaries of the 1790s, we find at least that he is not a freak without historical causes but that he responded to the common circumstances in ways markedly similar, sometimes even to odd details. But while fellow-poets soon left off their tentative efforts to evolve a system of "machinery" by which to come to terms with the epic events of their revolutionary era, Blake carried undauntedly on.

What, then, were the attributes shared by the chief poets of the 1790s, Blake, Wordsworth, Southey, Coleridge?—to whom I shall add, Shelley. Byron and Keats also had elements in common with their older contemporaries, but these lie outside the immediate scope of my paper. Shelley, however, though he matured in the cynical era of Napoleon and the English Regency, reiterated remarkably the pattern of his predecessors. By temperament he was more inclusively and extremely radical than anyone but Blake, and his early "principles," as he himself said, had "their origin from the discoveries which preceded and occasioned the revolutions of

[30] *Vala, or The Four Zoas*, I, 5, 21; IX, 827, 845.

America and France." That is, he had formed his mind on those writers, from Rousseau through Condorcet, Volney, Paine, and Godwin, whose ideas made up the climate of the 1790s—and also, it should be emphasized, on the King James Bible and *Paradise Lost*.[31]

1. First, these were all centrally political and social poets. It is by a peculiar injustice that Romanticism is often described as a mode of escapism, an evasion of the shocking changes, violence, and ugliness attending the emergence of the modern industrial and political world. The fact is that to a degree without parallel, even among major Victorian poets, these writers were obsessed with the realities of their era. Blake's wife mildly complained that her husband was always in Paradise; but from this vantage point he managed to keep so thoroughly in touch with mundane reality that, as David Erdman has demonstrated, his epics are hardly less steeped in the scenes and events of the day than is that latter-day epic, the *Ulysses* of James Joyce. Wordsworth said that he "had given twelve hours thought to the conditions and prospects of society, for one to poetry"; [32] Coleridge, Southey,

---

[31] *Proposals for an Association of Philanthropists* (1812), in *Shelley's Prose*, p. 67. Concerning the early formative influences on Shelley's thought, see K. N. Cameron, *The Young Shelley* (London, 1951). Mary Shelley testified that "in English, the Bible was [Shelley's] constant study," that the sublime poetry of the Old Testament "filled him with delight," and that over an extended period in 1816 and 1817, Shelley read both the Bible and *Paradise Lost* aloud to her (*The Complete Poetical Works of P. B. Shelley*, ed. Thomas Hutchinson [London, 1948], pp. 156, 536, 551). See Bennett Weaver, *Toward the Understanding of Shelley* (Ann Arbor, 1932).

[32] F. M. Todd, *Politics and the Poet: A Study of Wordsworth* (London, 1957), p. 11. Both of Wordsworth's long poems turn on an extended treatment of the French Revolution—in *The Prelude* as the crisis of his own

and Shelley could have made a claim similarly extravagant; all
these poets delivered themselves of political and social commentary in the form of prose-pamphlets, essays, speeches, editorials,
or sermons; and all exhibit an explicit or submerged concern
with the contemporary historical and intellectual situation in the
greater part of their verses, narrative, dramatic, and lyric, long
and short.

2. What obscures this concern is that in many poems the Romantics do not write direct political and moral commentary
but (in Schorer's apt phrase for Blake) "the politics of vision,"
uttered in the persona of the inspired prophet-priest. Neoclassic
poets had invoked the muse as a formality of the poetic ritual,
and the school of sensibility had expressed nostalgia for the
"diviner inspiration" of Spenser, Shakespeare, and Milton. But
when the Romantic poet asserts inspiration and revelation by a
power beyond himself—as Blake did repeatedly, or Shelley in
his claim that the great poets of his age are "the priests of an
unapprehended inspiration, the mirrors of gigantic shadows which
futurity casts upon the present" [33]—he means it. And when
Wordsworth called himself "A youthful Druid taught . . . Primeval mysteries, a Bard elect . . . a chosen Son," and Coleridge
characterized *The Prelude* as "More than historic, that prophetic
Lay," "An Orphic song" uttered by a "great Bard," [34] in an im-

---

life as exemplary poet, and in *The Excursion* as the crisis of his generation.
See also Carl R. Woodring, *Politics in the Poetry of Coleridge* (Madison,
1961), William Haller, *The Early Life of Robert Southey* (New York,
1917), and K. N. Cameron, *The Young Shelley*.

[33] For example, Blake's letter to Thomas Butts, April 25, 1803; Shelley,
"A Philosophical View of Reform," *Shelley's Prose*, p. 240.

[34] MS A, III, 82–93, in *William Wordsworth, The Prelude,* ed. Ernest

portant sense they meant it too, and we must believe that they meant it if we are to read them aright.

The Romantics, then, often spoke confidently as elected members of what Harold Bloom calls "The Visionary Company," the inspired line of singers from the prophets of the Old and New Testaments through Dante, Spenser, and above all Milton. For Milton had an exemplary role in this tradition as the native British (or Druidic) Bard who was a thorough political, social, and religious revolutionary, who claimed inspiration both from a Heavenly Muse and from the Holy Spirit that had supervised the Creation and inspired the biblical prophets, and who, after the failure of his millennial expectations from the English Revolution,[35] had kept his singing voice and salvaged his hope for mankind in an epic poem.

3. Following the Miltonic example, the Romantic poet of the 1790s tried to incorporate what he regarded as the stupendous events of the age in the suitably great poetic forms. He wrote, or planned to write an epic, or (like Milton in *Samson Agonistes*) emulated Aeschylean tragedy, or uttered visions combining the mode of biblical prophecy with the loose Pindaric, "the sublime" or "greater Ode," which by his eighteenth-century predecessors had been accorded a status next to epic, as peculiarly adapted to an enthusiastic and visionary imagination. Whatever the form, the Romantic Bard is one "who present, past, and future sees"; so that in dealing with current affairs his procedure is often

---

De Selincourt and Helen Darbishire (2d ed.; Oxford, 1959), p. 75; Coleridge, "To William Wordsworth," ll. 3, 45, 48.

[35] On Milton's millennialism see H. J. C. Grierson, *Milton and Wordsworth* (Cambridge, 1937), pp. 32–36.

panoramic, his stage cosmic, his agents quasi-mythological, and his logic of events apocalyptic. Typically this mode of Romantic vision fuses history, politics, philosophy, and religion into one grand design, by asserting Providence—or some form of natural teleology—to operate in the seeming chaos of human history so as to effect from present evil a greater good; and through the mid-1790s the French Revolution functions as the symptom or early stage of the abrupt culmination of this design, from which will emerge a new man on a new earth which is a restored Paradise.

To support these large generalizations I need to present a few particulars.

Robert Southey, the most matter-of-fact and worldly of these poets, said that his early adoration of Leonidas, hero of Thermopylae, his early study of Epictetus, "and the French Revolution at its height when I was just eighteen—by these my mind was moulded." [36] The first literary result came a year later, in 1793, when during six weeks of his long vacation from Oxford he wrote *Joan of Arc: An Epic Poem* [37]—with Blake's *French Revolution,* the first English epic worth historical notice since Glover's *Leonidas,* published in 1737. Southey's Joan has been called a Tom Paine in petticoats; she is also given to trances in which "strange events yet in the womb of Time" are to her "made manifest." In the first published version of 1796, Book IX consists of a sustained vision of the realms of hell and purgatory,

[36] Quoted by Edward Dowden, *Southey* (New York, 1880), p. 189.

[37] Southey's Preface to *Joan of Arc* (1837), *The Poetical Works of Robert Southey* (10 vols.; Boston, 1860), I, 11–12. The next year (1794), with even greater revolutionary élan, Southey dashed off in three mornings the Jacobin *Wat Tyler: A Drama* (*ibid.,* II, 28).

populated by the standard villains of the radicals' view of history. To Joan is revealed the Edenic past in the "blest aera of the infant world," and man's fall, through lust for gold and power, to this "theatre of woe"; yet "for the best/ Hath he ordained all things, the ALL-WISE!" because man, "Samson-like" shall "burst his fetters" in a violent spasm not quite named the French Revolution,

> and Earth shall once again
> Be Paradise, whilst WISDOM shall secure
> The state of bliss which IGNORANCE betrayed.
> "Oh age of happiness!" the Maid exclaim'd,
> "Roll fast thy current, Time, till that blest age
> Arrive!" [38]

To the second book of *Joan* Coleridge (then, like Southey, a Unitarian, and like both Southey and Wordsworth, considering entering the clergy) contributed what he called an "Epic Slice," which he soon patched up into an independent poem, *The Destiny*

---

[38] *Joan of Arc: An Epic Poem* (Bristol, 1796), Book I, ll. 497–99; Book IX, ll. 825–27, 837–72. In the MS version of 1793, the references to the French Revolution are explicit; see Book XI, ll. 633–749, in Benjamin W. Early, "Southey's *Joan of Arc*: The Unpublished Manuscript, the First Edition, and a Study of the Later Revisions" (MS doctoral thesis, Duke University Library, 1951). Southey wrote in 1830 that "forty years ago I could partake the hopes of those who expected that political revolutions were to bring about a political millennium" (*Correspondence with Caroline Bowles*, p. 200). By 1797, however, he seems to have been prepared to give back to Christ the task of realizing the dreams of Plato and Milton for total "happiness on earth": "Blessed hopes! awhile/ From man withheld, even to the latter days,/ When CHRIST shall come and all things be fulfill'd." ("Inscription IV. For the Apartment in Chepstow Castle," *Poems*, 1797.)

of Nations: A Vision. The vision, beamed "on the Prophet's
purgèd eye," reviews history, echoes the Book of Revelation, and
ends in the symbolic appearance of a bright cloud (the American
Revolution) and a brighter cloud (the French Revolution) from
which emerges "A dazzling form," obviously female, yet identified in Coleridge's note as an Apollo-figure, portending that
"Soon shall the Morning struggle into Day." [39] With the epo-
mania of the age, Coleridge considered writing an epic of his
own, laid out plans which would take twenty years to realize,
and let it go at that.[40] His ambition to be the Milton of his day
was, in practice, limited to various oracular odes, of which the
most interesting for our purpose is *Religious Musings,* his first
long poem in blank verse; on this, Coleridge said, "I build all my
poetic pretensions." [41] The poem as published bore the title "Religious Musings on Christmas Eve. In the year of Our Lord,
1794," and Coleridge had earlier called it "The Nativity." [42] The
year is precisely that of Blake's *Europe: A Prophecy,* and like
that poem, *Religious Musings* is clearly a revision for the time
being of Milton's "On the Morning of Christ's Nativity," which
had taken the occasion of memorializing Christ's birth to anticipate "The wakefull trump of doom" and the universal earthquake which will announce His Second Coming:

And then at last our bliss
Full and perfect is.

[39] "The Destiny of Nations," ll. 464, 326–38, 421–58. See Woodring,
Politics in the Poetry of Coleridge, pp. 169–73.
[40] To Joseph Cottle, April, 1797, in *Collected Letters,* ed. E. L. Griggs
(Oxford, 1956—), I, 320–21.
[41] *Collected Letters,* I, 197, 205.   [42] *Ibid.,* I, 147, 162 and footnote.

There is never any risk of mistaking Coleridge's voice for that of Blake, yet a reading of Coleridge's poem with Blake's in mind reveals how remarkably parallel were the effects of the same historical and literary situation, operating simultaneously on the imagination of the two poets.

Coleridge's opening, "This is the time," echoes "This is the Month" with which Milton begins his Prologue, as Blake's "The deep of winter came" reflects "It was the Winter wild" with which Milton begins the Hymn proper. (Blake's free verse is also at times reminiscent of the movement of Milton's marvelous stanza.) Musing on the significance of the First Advent, Coleridge says, "Behold a VISION gathers in my soul," which provides him, among other things, a survey of human history since "the primeval age" in the form of a brief theodicy, "all the sore ills" of "our mortal life" becoming "the immediate source/ Of mightier good." The future must bring "the fated day" of violent revolution by the oppressed masses, but happily "Philosophers and Bards" exist to mold the wild chaos "with plastic might" into the "perfect forms" of their own inspired visions. Coleridge then presents an interpretation of contemporary affairs which, following his Unitarian mentor, Joseph Priestley, he neatly summarizes in his prose "Argument" as: "The French Revolution. Millennium. Universal Redemption. Conclusion." His procedure is to establish a parallel (developed in elaborate footnotes) between current revolutionary events and the violent prophecies of the Book of Revelation. The machinery of apocalypse is allegorical, with the "Giant Frenzy" given the function of Blake's Orc in "Uprooting empires with his whirlwind arm." In due course the "blest future rushes on my view!" in the form of humankind as a "vast family of Love" living in a communist economy. "The mighty Dead" awaken, and

> To Milton's trump
> The high groves of the renovated Earth
> Unbosom their glad echoes,

in the adoring presence of three English interpreters of millennial prophecy, Newton, Hartley, and Priestley, "patriot, and saint, and sage." [43] (In Blake's *Europe,* not Milton but Newton had "siez'd the trump & blow'd the enormous blast"; as in Coleridge's poem, however, he seemingly appears not in his capacity as scientist but as author of a commentary on the Book of Revelation.)

Wordsworth thought the concluding section of *Religious Musings* on "the renovated Earth" to be the best in Coleridge's *Poems* of 1796. On this subject Wordsworth was an expert, for a year prior to the writing of the poem, in 1793, he had concluded his own *Descriptive Sketches* with the prophecy (precisely matching the prophecy he attributed to the Wanderer in his *Excursion*) that the wars consequent on the French Revolution would fulfill the predictions both of the Book of Revelation and of Virgil's Fourth Eclogue:

[43] *Complete Poetical Works,* ed. E. H. Coleridge (2 vols.; Oxford, 1912), I, 108–23, and notes. David Hartley had included his interpretation of millennial prophecy in his *Observations on Man,* Part II, Sections IV and V. In ll. 126–58 of *Religious Musings* Coleridge, like Blake in his later prophecies, interpreted the fall of man as a splintering of social fraternity into anarchic individuality, and his redemption at the Second Coming as a rejunction of separate selves into a single "Self, that no alien knows!" Cf. the opening of Blake's *The Four Zoas,* I, 9–23.

—Tho' Liberty shall soon, indignant, raise
Red on his hills his beacon's comet blaze . . .
Yet, yet rejoice, tho' Pride's perverted ire
Rouze Hell's own aid, and wrap thy hills in fire.
Lo! from th' innocuous flames, a lovely birth!
With its own Virtues springs another earth:
Nature, as in her prime, her virgin reign
Begins, and Love and Truth compose her train . . .
No more . . .
On his pale horse shall fell Consumption go.

"How is it," Blake was to ask in his conclusion of *The Four Zoas*, "we have walk'd thro' fires & yet are not consum'd?/ How is it that all things are chang'd, even as in ancient times?" [44]
Some two decades later Shelley recapitulated and expanded these poetic manifestations of the earlier 1790s. At the age of nineteen he began his first long poem, *Queen Mab*, in the mode of a vision of the woeful past, the ghastly present, and the blissful future, and although the concepts are those of the French and English *philosophes*, and the Spirit of Necessity replaces Providence as the agent of redemption, much of the imagery is imported from biblical millennialism. The prophecy is that "A garden shall arise, in loveliness/ Surpassing fabled Eden"; when

[44] *Descriptive Sketches* (1793 version), ll. 774–91. Blake, *The Four Zoas*, IX, 844–45; see also *America*, VIII, 15. For Wordsworth's opinion of the apocalyptic passage in Coleridge's *Religious Musings* see Coleridge's *Collected Letters*, I, 215–16. As late as 1808 the Spanish insurrection against Napoleon revived Wordsworth's millennial hopes: "We trust that Regeneration is at hand: these are works of recovered innocence and wisdom . . . *redeunt Saturnia regna*" (Wordsworth, *The Convention of Cintra*, ed. A. V. Dicey [London, 1915], p. 122; also pp. 10–11).

it eventuates, "All things are recreated," the lion sports "in the sun/ Beside the dreadless kid," and man's intellectual and moral nature participates in "The gradual renovation" until he stands "with taintless body and mind" in a "happy earth! reality of Heaven!" the "consummation of all mortal hope!" [45]

If I may just glance over the fence of my assigned topic: in Germany, as in England, a coincidence of historical, religious, and literary circumstances produced a comparable imaginative result. In the early 1790s the young Hölderlin was caught up in the intoxication of the revolutionary promise; he was at the time a student of theology at Tübingen, and immersed in the literary tradition of *Sturm und Drang* libertarianism, Schiller's early poems, and Klopstock's *Messias* and allegoric odes. A number of Hölderlin's odes of that decade (the two "Hymnen an die Freiheit," the "Hymne an die Menschheit," "Der Zeitgeist") are notably parallel to the English form I have been describing; that is, they are visionary, oracular, panoramic, and see history on the verge of a blessed culmination in which the French Revolution is the crucial event, the Book of Revelation the chief model, and the agencies a combination of Greek divinities, biblical symbols, and abstract personifications of his own devising. In the "Hymne an die Freiheit" of 1792, for example, the rapt poet chants a revelation of man's first pastoral innocence, love, and happiness; this "Paradise" is destroyed by a "curse"; but then in response to a call by the Goddess Liberty, Love "reconciles the long discord" and inaugurates "the new hour of creation" of a free, fraternal, abundantly vital, and radiant century in which

[45] *Queen Mab,* IV, 88–89; VIII, 107 ff.; IX, 1–4.

"the ancient infamy is cancelled" and "der Erndte grosser Tag beginnt"—"there begins the great day of the harvest."[46]

IV. THE APOCALYPSE OF IMAGINATION

The visionary poems of the earlier 1790s and Shelley's earlier prophecies show imaginative audacity and invention, but they are not, it must be confessed, very good poems. The great Romantic poems were written not in the mood of revolutionary exaltation but in the later mood of revolutionary disillusionment or despair. Many of the great poems, however, do not break with the formative past, but continue to exhibit, in a transformed but recognizable fashion, the scope, the poetic voice, the design, the ideas, and the imagery developed in the earlier period. This continuity of tradition converts what would otherwise be a literary curiosity into a matter of considerable historical interest, and helps us to identify and interpret some of the strange but characteristic elements in later Romantic enterprises.

Here is one out of many available instances. It will have become apparent even from these brief summaries that certain terms, images, and quasi-mythical agents tend to recur and to assume a specialized reference to revolutionary events and expectations: the earthquake and the volcano, the purging fire, the emerging sun, the dawn of glad day, the awakening earth

[46] Hölderlin, *Sämtliche Werke,* ed. Friedrich Beissner (Stuttgart, 1946—), Vol. I, Part I, pp. 139–42. See Geneviève Bianquis, "Hölderlin et la révolution française," *Études Germaniques,* VII (1952), 105–16, and Maurice Delorme, *Hölderlin et la révolution française* (Monaco, 1959). The relevance of Hölderlin was pointed out to me by my colleague, Paul De Man.

in springtime, the Dionysian figure of revolutionary destruction and the Apollonian figure of the promise of a bright new order. Prominent among these is a term which functions as one of the principal leitmotifs of Romantic literature. To Europe at the end of the eighteenth century the French Revolution brought what St. Augustine said Christianity had brought to the ancient world: hope. As Coleridge wrote, on first hearing Wordsworth's *Prelude* read aloud, the poet sang of his experience "Amid the tremor of a realm aglow,"

> When from the general heart of human kind
> Hope sprang forth like a full-born Deity!

and afterward, "Of that dear Hope afflicted and struck down. . . ." [47] This is no ordinary human hope, but a universal, absolute, and novel hope which sprang forth from the Revolutionary events sudden and complete, like Minerva. Pervasively in both the verse and prose of the period, "hope," with its associated term, "joy," and its opposites, "dejection," "despondency," and "despair," are used in a special application, as shorthand for the limitless faith in human and social possibility aroused by the Revolution, and its reflex, the nadir of feeling caused by its seeming failure—as Wordsworth had put it, the "utter loss of hope itself/ And things to hope for." (*The Prelude*, 1805, XI, 6–7.)

[47] "To William Wordsworth," ll. 34–38. Cf., e.g., *The Prelude* (1805), II, 448–66, X, 355–81, 690–728; *The Excursion*, II, 210–23; *The Convention of Cintra*, pp. 10–11, 157–58, 187–88; Shelley, Preface to *The Revolt of Islam, Poetical Works*, pp. 33–34; Hazlitt, *Complete Works*, IV, 119–20, XVII, 196–98, 316, and his *Life of Thomas Holcroft*, ed. Elbridge Colby (2 vols.; London, 1925), II, 92–93.

It is not irrelevant, I believe, that many seemingly apolitical poems of the later Romantic period turn on the theme of hope and joy and the temptation to abandon all hope and fall into dejection and despair; the recurrent emotional pattern is that of the key books of *The Excursion,* labeled "Despondency" and "Despondency Corrected," which apply specifically to the failure of millennial hope in the Revolution. But I want to apply this observation to one of those passages in *The Prelude* where Wordsworth suddenly breaks through to a prophetic vision of the hidden significance of the literal narrative. In the sixth book Wordsworth describes his first tour of France with Robert Jones in the summer of 1790, the brightest period of the Revolution. The mighty forms of Nature, "seizing a youthful fancy," had already "given a charter to irregular hopes," but now all Europe

was thrilled with joy,
France standing on the top of golden hours,
And human nature seeming born again.

Sharing the universal intoxication, "when joy of one" was "joy for tens of millions," they join in feasting and dance with a "blithe host/ Of Travellers" returning from the Federation Festival at Paris, "the great spousals newly solemnised/ At their chief city, in the sight of Heaven." In his revisions of the 1805 version of *The Prelude,* Wordsworth inserted at this point a passage in which he sees, with anguished foreboding, the desecration by French troops of the Convent of the Chartreuse (an event which did not take place until two years later, in 1792). The travelers' way then brings them to the Simplon Pass.

Wordsworth's earlier account of this tour in the *Descriptive*

Sketches, written mainly in 1791–92, had ended with the prophecy of a new earth emerging from apocalyptic fires, and a return to the golden age. Now, however, he describes a strange access of sadness, a "melancholy slackening." On the Simplon road they had left their guide and climbed ever upward, until a peasant told them that they had missed their way and that the course now lay downwards.

> Loth to believe what we so grieved to hear,
> For still we had hopes that pointed to the clouds,
> We questioned him again, and yet again;

but every reply "Ended in this,—*that we had crossed the Alps.*"

> Imagination . . .
> That awful Power rose from the mind's abyss
> Like an unfathered vapour that enwraps,
> At once, some lonely traveller; I was lost;
> Halted without an effort to break through;
> But to my conscious soul I now can say—
> "I recognise thy glory". . . .

Only now, in retrospect, does he recognize that his imagination had penetrated to the emblematic quality of the literal climb, in a revelation proleptic of the experience he was to recount in all the remainder of *The Prelude.* Man's infinite hopes can never be matched by the world as it is and man as he is, for these exhibit a discrepancy no less than that between his "hopes that pointed to the clouds" and the finite height of the Alpine pass. But in the magnitude of the disappointment lies its consolation;

for the flash of vision also reveals that infinite longings are inherent in the human spirit, and that the gap between the inordinacy of his hope and the limits of possibility is the measure of man's dignity and greatness:

Our destiny, our being's heart and home,
Is with infinitude, and only there;
With hope it is, hope that can never die,
Effort, and expectation, and desire,
And something evermore about to be.

In short, Wordsworth evokes from the unbounded and hence impossible hopes in the French Revolution a central Romantic doctrine; one which reverses the cardinal neoclassic ideal of setting only accessible goals, by converting what had been man's tragic error—the inordinacy of his "pride" that persists in setting infinite aims for finite man—into his specific glory and his triumph. Wordsworth shares the recognition of his fellow-Romantics, German and English, of the greatness of man's infinite *Sehnsucht*, his saving insatiability, Blake's "I want! I want!" [48] Shelley's "the desire of the moth for the star"; but with a characteristic and unique difference, as he goes on at once to reveal:

[48] It is an interesting coincidence that Blake's "I want! I want!" (which is illustrated by a man climbing a ladder reaching to the moon) was his retort to a political cartoon by Gillray caricaturing the inordinacy of revolutionary hope, by depicting a short ladder pointing futilely toward the moon. See Erdman, *Blake, Prophet Against Empire*, pp. 186–88. The parable, in its political application, was a familiar one; thus Edmund Burke had said (1780): "If we cry, like children, for the moon, like children we must cry on" (*The Works of the Right Honorable Edmund Burke* [12 vols., London, 1899], II, 357).

Under such banners militant, the soul
Seeks for no trophies, struggles for no spoils
That may attest her prowess, blest in thoughts
That are their own perfection and reward. . . .

The militancy of overt political action has been transformed into
the paradox of spiritual quietism: under such militant banners
is no march, but a wise passiveness. This truth having been revealed to him, Wordsworth at once goes on to his apocalypse of
nature in the Simplon Pass, where the *coincidentia oppositorum*
of its physical attributes become the symbols of the biblical Book
of Revelation:

Characters of the great Apocalypse,
The types and symbols of Eternity,
Of first, and last, and midst, and without end.[49]

This and its companion passages in *The Prelude* enlighten the
orphic darkness of Wordsworth's "Prospectus" for *The Recluse,*
drafted as early as 1800, when *The Prelude* had not yet been
differentiated from the larger poem. Wordsworth's aim, he there
reveals, is still that of the earlier period of millennial hope in
revolution, still expressed in a fusion of biblical and classical

[49] *The Prelude* (1850), VI, 322–640. On the glory of infinite promise
aroused by the Revolution see also *ibid.,* XI, 105–23. Wordsworth's later
revision of the passage of apocalyptic hope in the *Descriptive Sketches* of
1793 parallels the emblematic significance of the Alpine crossing:

Lo, from the flames a great and glorious birth;
As if a new-made heaven were hailing a new earth!
—All cannot be: the promise is too fair
For creatures doomed to breathe terrestrial air. . . .
                                    (*Poetical Works,* I, 89)

imagery. Evil is to be redeemed by a regained Paradise, or
Elysium: "Paradise," he says, "and groves/ Elysian, Fortunate
Fields . . . why should they be/ A history only of departed
things?" And the restoration of Paradise, as in the Book of Revelation, is still symbolized by a sacred marriage. But the hope has
been shifted from the history of mankind to the mind of the
single individual, from militant external action to an imaginative
act; and the marriage between the Lamb and the New Jerusalem
has been converted into a marriage between subject and object,
mind and nature, which creates a new world out of the old world
of sense:

> For the discerning intellect of Man,
> When wedded to this goodly universe
> In love and holy passion, shall find these
> A simple produce of the common day.
> —I, long before the blissful hour arrives,
> Would chant, in lonely peace, the spousal verse
> Of this great consummation . . .
> And the creation (by no lower name
> Can it be called) which they with blended might
> Accomplish:—this is our high argument.[50]

In the other Romantic visionaries, as in Wordsworth, naive millennialism produced mainly declamation, but the shattered trust
in premature political revolution and the need to reconstitute the
grounds of hope lay behind the major achievements. And something close to Wordsworth's evolution—the shift to a spiritual
and moral revolution which will transform our experience of

[50] *Poetical Works,* ed. De Selincourt, V, 3–5.

the old world—is also the argument of a number of the later writings of Blake, Coleridge, Shelley, and, with all his differences, Hölderlin. An example from Shelley must suffice. Most of Shelley's large enterprises after *Queen Mab—The Revolt of Islam, Prometheus Unbound, Hellas*—were inspired by a later recrudescence of the European revolutionary movement. Shelley's view of human motives and possibilities became more and more tragic, and, like Blake after his *French Revolution,* he moved from the bald literalism of *Queen Mab* to an imaginative form increasingly biblical, symbolic, and mythic; but the theme continues to be the ultimate promise of a renovation in human nature and circumstances. In *Prometheus Unbound* this event is symbolized by the reunion of Prometheus and Asia in a joyous ceremony in which all the cosmos participates. But this new world is one which reveals itself to the purged imagination of Man when he has reformed his moral nature at its deep and twisted roots; and the last words of Demogorgon, the inscrutable agent of this apocalypse, describe a revolution of spirit whose sole agencies are the cardinal virtues of endurance, forgiveness, love, and, above all, hope—though a hope that is now hard to distinguish from despair:

To suffer woes which Hope thinks infinite . . .
To love, and bear; to hope till Hope creates
From its own wreck the thing it contemplates . . .
This is alone Life, Joy, Empire, and Victory!

V. WORDSWORTH'S OTHER VOICE

"Two voices are there. . . . And, Wordsworth, both are thine." I have as yet said nothing about Wordsworth's *Lyrical*

Ballads and related poems, although Hazlitt regarded these as the inauguration of a new poetic era and the close poetic equivalent to the revolutionary politics of the age. Yet the *Ballads* seem in every way antithetical to the poetry I have just described: instead of displaying a panoramic vision of present, past, and future in an elevated oracular voice, these poems undertake to represent realistic "incidents and situations from common life" in ordinary language and to employ "humble and rustic life" as the main source of the simple characters and the model for the plain speech.

Here are some of the reasons Hazlitt gives for his claim that "the political changes of the day were the model on which [Wordsworth] formed and conducted his poetical experiments":

> His Muse (it cannot be denied, and without this we cannot explain its character at all) is a levelling one. It proceeds on a principle of equality, and strives to reduce all things to the same standard. . . .
>
> His popular, inartificial style gets rid (at a blow) of all the trappings of verse, of all the high places of poetry. . . . We begin *de novo,* on a tabula rasa of poetry. . . . The distinctions of rank, birth, wealth, power . . . are not to be found here. . . . The harp of Homer, the trump of Pindar and of Alcaeus, are still.[51]

---

[51] *The Spirit of the Age, Complete Works,* XI, 87. Cf. "On the Living Poets," *ibid.,* V, 161–64. Christopher Wordsworth, though his loyalties were the polar opposites of Hazlitt's, also accounted for the theory of *Lyrical Ballads* in political terms: "The clue to his *poetical* theory, in some of its questionable details, may be found in his *political* principles; these had been democratical, and still, though in some degree modified, they were

Making due allowance for his love of extravagance, I think that Hazlitt makes out a very plausible case. He shrewdly recognizes that Wordsworth's criteria are as much social as literary, and that by their egalitarianism they subvert the foundations of a view of poetry inherited from the Renaissance. This view assumed and incorporated a hierarchical structure of social classes. In its strict form, it conceived poetry as an order of well-defined genres, controlled by a theory of decorum whereby the higher poetic kinds represent primarily kings and the aristocracy, the humbler classes (in other than a subsidiary function) are relegated to the lowlier forms, and each poem is expressed in a level of style —high, middle, or low—appropriate, among other things, to the social status of its characters and the dignity of its genre. In England after the sixteenth century, this system had rarely been held with continental rigor, and eighteenth-century critics and poets had carried far the work of breaking down the social distinctions built into a poetic developed for an aristocratic audience. But Wordsworth's practice, buttressed by a strong critical manifesto, carried an existing tendency to an extreme which Hazlitt regarded as a genuine innovation, an achieved revolution against the *ancien régime* in literature. He is, Hazlitt said, "the most original poet now living, and the one whose writings could least be spared: for they have no substitute elsewhere." And Wordsworth has not only leveled, he has transvalued Renaissance and neoclassic aesthetics, by deliberately seeking out the ignominious, the delinquent, and the social outcast as subjects for serious or tragic consideration—not only, Hazlitt noted, "peasants, pedlars,

---

of a republican character." (*Memoirs of William Wordsworth* [2 vols., Boston, 1851], I, 127.)

and village-barbers," but also "convicts, female vagrants, gipsies . . . ideot boys and mad mothers." [52] Hence the indignation of Lord Byron, who combined political liberalism with a due regard for aristocratic privilege and traditional poetic decorum:

> "Peddlers," and "Boats," and "Wagons"! Oh! ye shades
> Of Pope and Dryden, are we come to this?

In his Preface to *Lyrical Ballads* Wordsworth justified his undertaking mainly by the ultimate critical sanctions then available, of elemental and permanent "nature" as against the corruptions and necessarily short-lived fashions of "art." But Wordsworth also dealt with the genesis and rationale of *Lyrical Ballads* in several other writings, and in terms broader than purely critical, and these passages clearly relate his poems of humble lives in the plain style to his concept and practice of poetry in the grand oracular style.

In the crucial thirteenth book of *The Prelude* Wordsworth describes how, trained "to meekness" and exalted by "humble faith," he turned from disillusionment with the "sublime/ In what the Historian's pen so much delights/ To blazon," to "fraternal love" for "the unassuming things that hold/ A silent station in this beauteous world," and so to a surrogate for his lost revolutionary hopes:

> The promise of the present time retired
> Into its true proportion; sanguine schemes,
> Ambitious projects, pleased me less; I sought

[52] *Complete Works,* XI, 89, V, 162–63. On the novelty of Wordsworth's poems see also V, 156, and XVII, 117.

For present good in life's familiar face,
And built thereon my hopes of good to come.

He turned, that is, away from Man as he exists only in the hopes
of naive millennialists or the abstractions of the philosophers
of perfectibility to "the man whom we behold/ With our own
eyes"; and especially to the humble and obscure men of the
lower and rural classes, "who live/ By bodily toil," free from
the "artificial lights" of urban upper-class society, and utter the
spontaneous overflow of powerful feelings ("Expressing liveliest
thoughts in lively words/ As native passion dictates"). "Of these,
said I, shall be my song." But, he insists, in this new subject he
continues to speak "things oracular," for though he is "the
humblest," he stands in the great line of the "Poets, even as
Prophets, each with each/ Connected in a mighty scheme of
truth," each of whom possesses "his own peculiar faculty,/
Heaven's gift, a sense that fits him to perceive/ Objects unseen
before." And chief among the prophetic insights granted to
Wordsworth is the discovery that Nature has the power to
"consecrate" and "to breathe/ Grandeur upon the very humblest
face/ Of human life," as well as upon the works of man, even
when these are "mean, have nothing lofty of their own." [53]

We come here to a central paradox among the various ones
that lurk in the oracular passages of Wordsworth's major period:
the oxymoron of the humble-grand, the lofty-mean, the trivial-
sublime—as Hazlitt recognized when he said that Wordsworth's
Muse "is distinguished by a proud humility," and that he "elevates
the mean" and endeavors "(not in vain) to aggrandise the

[53] *The Prelude* (1850), XIII, 11–312.

trivial." [54] The ultimate source of this concept is, I think, obvious, and Wordsworth several times plainly points it out for us. Thus in *The Ruined Cottage* (1797–98) the Pedlar (whose youthful experiences parallel Wordsworth's, as the poet showed by later transferring a number of passages to *The Prelude*) had first studied the Scriptures, and only afterward had come to *"feel* his faith" by discovering the corresponding symbol-system, "the writing," in the great book of nature, where "the least of things/ Seemed infinite," so that (as a "chosen son") his own "being thus became/ Sublime and comprehensive. . . . Yet was his heart/ Lowly"; he also learned to recognize in the simple people of rural life what Wordsworth in a note called "the aristocracy of nature." [55] The ultimate source of Wordsworth's discovery, that is, was the Bible, and especially the New Testament, which is grounded on the radical paradox that "the last shall be first," and dramatizes that fact in the central mystery of God incarnate as a lowly carpenter's son who takes fishermen for his disciples, consorts with beggars, publicans, and fallen women, and dies ignominiously, crucified with thieves. This interfusion of highest and lowest, the divine and the base, as Erich Auerbach has shown, had from the beginning been a stumbling-block to readers habituated to the classical separation of levels of subject-matter and style, and Robert Lowth in the mid-eighteenth century still found it necessary to insist, as had Augustine and other theologians almost a millennium and a half earlier, that the style of the

[54] *Complete Works*, XI, 87–89.
[55] "The Ruined Cottage," in *Poetical Works*, V, 379 ff., ll. 53–59, 145–66, 264–75; and p. 411, note to l. 341 of the revised version in *The Excursion*, Book I.

Bible had its special propriety and was genuinely sublime, and
not, as it seemed to a cultivated taste, indecorous, vulgar, bar-
barous, grotesque.[56] Wordsworth, it should be recalled, had had
a pious mother, attended a church school at Hawkeshead, and
was intended for the clergy. In this aspect his poetic reflects a
movement in eighteenth-century pietism and evangelicalism
which had emphasized, in the theological term, God's "condescension" or "accommodation" in revealing his immense divinity to the limited human mind through the often trivial events
of Scripture, as well as in sending his son to be born as the
lowliest among men. The archetypal figure, among Wordsworth's
many numinous solitaries, is the humble shepherd magnified in
the mist, "glorified" by the setting sun, and "descried in distant
sky,"

> A solitary object and sublime,
> Above all height! like an aerial cross
> Stationed alone upon a spiry rock
> Of the Chartreuse, for worship. Thus was man
> Ennobled outwardly before my sight—

apotheosized, rather, as *figura Christi,* the Good Shepherd himself; for by such means Wordsworth learned, he says, to see Man

[56] Robert Lowth, *Lectures on the Sacred Poetry of the Hebrews* (1753)
(London, 1847), pp. 79–84 and *passim.* On earlier theological discussions
of the Christian paradox of *humilitas-sublimitas,* see Erich Auerbach,
Mimesis (Princeton, 1953), pp. 72–73, 151–55, "Sermo Humilis," *Romanische Forschungen,* LXIV (1952), 304–64, and "St. Francis of Assisi
in Dante's *Commedia,*" in *Scenes from the Drama of European Literature*
(New York, 1959), pp. 79–98; also Joseph Mazzeo, "St. Augustine's Rhetoric of Silence," *Journal of the History of Ideas,* XXIII (1962), 183 ff.

"As, more than anything we know, instinct/ With godhead,"
while yet "acknowledging dependency sublime." [57]

An important document connecting the religious, political, and
aesthetic elements in his poetic theory is Wordsworth's neglected
"Essay, Supplementary to the Preface" of 1815, in which he undertakes to explain at length why his *Lyrical Ballads* had been met
with almost "unremitting hostility" ever since they appeared. The
argument is extraordinarily contorted, even for Wordsworth's
prose; but this, I believe, is the gist of it. "The higher poetry,"
especially when it "breathes the spirit of religion," unites "grandeur" and "simplicity," and in consequence is apt to evoke dislike, contempt, suspicion from the reader.

> For when Christianity, the religion of humility, is founded
> upon the proudest faculty of our nature [imagination], what
> can be expected but contradictions? . . .
>
> The commerce between Man and His Maker cannot be
> carried on but by a process where much is represented in little,
> and the Infinite Being accommodates himself to a finite ca-
> pacity. In all this may be perceived the affinity between religion
> and poetry.

(In the sentence before the last, Wordsworth defines exactly the
theological concept of "accommodation" or "condescension.")

[57] *The Prelude* (1850), VIII, 256–76, 492–94. Cf. Philippians 2:7–9:
Christ took on "the form of a servant" and "humbled himself" even unto
"the death of the cross. Wherefore God also hath highly exalted him. . . ."
See also, e.g., Matthew 23:11–12 and I Corinthians 1:27–28. On the history
of the theological concept of "condescensio," with special reference to the
eighteenth century, see Karlfried Gründer, *Figur und Geschichte* (Frei-
burg/Munich, 1958).

Wordsworth then puts himself at the end of a long list of great
poets who had been neglected or misunderstood; necessarily so,
for original genius consists in doing well "what was never done
before," and so introducing "a new element into the intellectual
universe"; hence such an author has "the task of *creating* the
taste by which he is to be enjoyed." Wordsworth's originality,
he says (Hazlitt made essentially the same claim), lies in producing a revolutionary mode of sublimity in poetry. Can it,
then,

> be wondered that there is little existing preparation for a poet
> charged with a new mission to extend its kingdom [i.e., of
> sublimity] and to augment and spread its enjoyments?

The "instinctive wisdom" and "heroic" (that is, epic) "passions"
of the ancients have united in his heart "with the meditative
wisdom of later ages" (that is, of the Christian era) to produce
the imaginative mode of "sublimated humanity," and *"there,*
the poet must reconcile himself for a season to few and scattered
hearers." For he must create the taste by which his innovation
is to be enjoyed by stripping from the reader's literary responses
their ingrained class-consciousness and social snobbery—what
Wordsworth calls "the prejudices of false refinement," "pride,"
and "vanity"—so as to establish "that dominion over the spirits
of readers by which they are to be humbled and humanised, in
order that they may be purified and exalted." [58] Having given

---

[58] "Essay, Supplementary to the Preface" of 1815, in *Poetical Works,* II,
411–29. Cf. the letter to J. K. Miller, Dec. 17, 1831. De Quincey agreed
with Wordsworth (and Hazlitt) that the *Lyrical Ballads* were without
literary precedent: "I found in these poems . . . an absolute revelation of
untrodden worlds . . ." (*Collected Writings,* II, 139).

up the hope of revolutionizing the social and political structure, Wordsworth has discovered that his new calling, his divine "mission," condemning him to a period of inevitable neglect and scorn, is to effect through his poetry an egalitarian revolution of the spirit (what he elsewhere calls "an entire regeneration" of his upper-class readers) [59] so that they may share his revelation of the equivalence of souls, the heroic dimensions of common life, and the grandeur of the ordinary and the trivial in Nature.

In his account of this same discovery in *The Prelude*, Book XIII, Wordsworth says that in his exercise of a special power, unprecedented in literature, "Upon the vulgar forms of present things,/ The actual world of our familiar days,"

> I remember well
> That in life's every-day appearances
> I seemed about this time to gain clear sight
> Of a new world,

capable of being made visible "to other eyes," which is the product of "A balance, an ennobling interchange," between "the object seen, and eye that sees." [60] This carries us back to the "Prospectus" to *The Recluse*, for it is clear that this "new world" is an aspect of the re-created universe there represented as "A simple produce of the common day," if only we learn to marry our mind to nature "In love and holy passion." And if we put the "Prospectus" back into its original context in the concluding

[59] In a letter to Lady Beaumont, May 21, 1807, on the same subject as the "Essay Supplementary," in *Wordsworth's Literary Criticism*, ed. Nowell C. Smith (London, 1905), p. 54.

[60] *The Prelude* (1850), XIII, 352–78.

section of *Home at Grasmere,* we find that this document, written precisely at the turn of the century, gathers together the various themes with which we have been dealing: the sense of divine mission and illumination, the conversion of his aspiration for millennial achievements beyond possibility into its spiritual equivalent in a militant quietism, and the replacement of his epic schemes by a new poetic enterprise, to communicate his transforming vision of the common man and the ordinary universe.

In the seclusion of Grasmere vale, Wordsworth has dismissed "all Arcadian dreams,/ All golden fancies of the golden Age" that is "to be/ Ere time expire," yet finds remaining a "sufficient hope." He proclaims that "yet to me I feel/ That an internal brightness is vouchsafed," something that "is shared by none," which impels him, "divinely taught," to speak "Of what in man is human or divine." The voice of Reason sanctions the lesson which Nature has stealthily taught him:

> Be mild and cleave to gentle things,
> Thy glory and thy happiness be there.
> Nor fear, though thou confide in me, a want
> Of aspirations that *have* been, of foes
> To wrestle with, and victory to complete,
> Bounds to be leapt, darkness to be explored . . .
> All shall survive—though changed their office. . . .

Therefore he bids "farewell to the Warrior's schemes," as well as to "that other hope, long mine, the hope to fill/ The heroic trumpet with the Muse's breath!" But having given up his ambition for a Miltonic epic, he at once finds that his new argument exceeds in its scope the height of Milton's "heaven of heavens" and the depths of Milton's hell, and that it presents its imaginative equivalent of a restored Paradise. Hence he will need, he claims —in that union of arrogance with humility which characterizes all poet-prophets who know they are inspired, but by a power for which they are not responsible—a Muse that will outsoar Milton's, just as Milton had claimed that his Muse would outsoar "th' Aonian Mount" of the pagan Homer. "Urania," Wordsworth says,

> I shall need
> Thy guidance, or a greater Muse, if such
> Descend to earth or dwell in highest heaven! [61]

Wordsworth, then, in the period beginning about 1797, came to see his destiny to lie in spiritual rather than in overt action and adventure, and to conceive his radical poetic vocation to consist in communicating his unique and paradoxical, hence inevitably misunderstood, revelation of the more-than-heroic grandeur of the humble, the contemned, the ordinary, and the trivial, whether in the plain style of direct ballad-like representation, or in the elevated voice in which he presents himself in his office as recipient of this gift of vision. In either case, the mode in which Wordsworth conceived his mission evolved out of the ambition to participate in the renovation of the world and of man which he had shared with his fellow-poets during the period of revolutionary enthusiasm. Both the oracular and the plain poetry, in the last analysis, go back beyond Milton, to that inexhaustible source of radical thought, the Bible—the oracular poetry to the

---

[61] *Home at Grasmere* (1800), in *Poetical Works,* V, 334 ff., ll. 625-34, 664-750; "Prospectus," ll. 25-71.

Old Testament prophets and their descendant, the author of the Book of Revelation, and the plain poetry to the story of Christ and to His pronouncements on the exaltation of the lowly and the meek. For the Jesus of the New Testament, as the Reverend Mark Wilks had said in 1791, was indeed "a revolutionary," though not a political one; and Wordsworth, in his long career as apologist for the Anglican Establishment, never again came so close to the spirit of primitive Christianity as in the latter 1790s when, according to Coleridge, he had been still "a Republican & at least a *Semi*-atheist." [62]

[62] To John Thelwall, May 13, 1796, *Collected Letters,* I, 216.

Lionel Trilling

THE FATE OF PLEASURE:

WORDSWORTH TO DOSTOEVSKY

OF ALL critical essays in the English language, there is none that has established itself so firmly in our minds as Wordsworth's Preface to *Lyrical Ballads*. Indeed, certain of the statements that the Preface makes about the nature of poetry have come to exist for us as something like proverbs of criticism. This is deplorable, for the famous utterances, in the form in which we hold them in memory, can only darken counsel. A large part of the literate world believes that Wordsworth defines poetry as the spontaneous overflow of powerful feelings. With such a definition we shall not get very far in our efforts to think about poetry, and in point of fact Wordsworth makes no such definition. Much less does he say, as many find it convenient to recall, that poetry is emotion recollected in tranquillity. Yet the tenacity with which we hold in mind our distortions of what Wordsworth actually does say suggests the peculiar power of the essay as a whole, its unique existence as a work of criticism. Its cogency in argument is notable, even if intermittent, but the Preface is not regarded by its readers only as an argument. By reason of its eloquence, and because of the impetuous spirit with which it engages the great questions of the nature and function of poetry, it presents itself to us not chiefly as a discourse, but rather as a dramatic action, and we are prepared to respond to its utterances less for their truth than for their happy boldness.

This being so, it should be a matter for surprise that one especially bold utterance of the Preface has not engaged us at all and is scarcely ever cited. I refer to the sentence in which Wordsworth speaks of what he calls "the grand elementary principle of pleasure," and says of it that it constitutes "the naked and native dignity of man," that it is the principle by which man "knows, and feels, and lives, and moves."

This is a statement which has great intrinsic interest, because, if we recognize that it is bold at all, we must also perceive that it is bold to the point of being shocking, for it echoes and it controverts St. Paul's sentence which tells us that "we live, and move, and have our being" in God. (Acts 17:28.) And in addition to its intrinsic interest, it has great historical interest, not only because it sums up a characteristic tendency of eighteenth-century thought but also because it bears significantly upon a characteristic tendency of our contemporary culture. Its relation to our contemporary culture is chiefly a negative one—our present sense of life does not accommodate the idea of pleasure as something which constitutes the "naked and native dignity of man."

The word *pleasure* occurs frequently in the Preface. Like earlier writers on the subject, when Wordsworth undertakes to explain why we do, or should, value poetry, he bases his explanation upon the pleasure which poetry gives. Generally he uses the word in much the same sense that was intended by his predecessors. The pleasure which used commonly to be associated with poetry was morally unexceptionable and not very intense—it was generally understood that poetry might indeed sometimes excite the mind but only as a step toward composing it. But the word has, we know, two separate moral ambiences and two very different degrees of intensity. The pleasures of domestic life are virtuous; the pleasures of Imagination or Melancholy propose the idea of a cultivated delicacy of mind in those who experience them; the name of an English pipe-tobacco, "Parson's Pleasure," suggests how readily the word consorts with ideas of mildness. None of these propose what Byron had in mind when he wrote, "O pleasure! you're indeed a pleasant thing,/ Although one must be damn'd for you no doubt." The *Oxford English Dictionary* takes due note of what it calls an "unfavorable" sense of the word: "Sensuous enjoyment as a chief object of life, or end, in itself" and informs us that in this pejorative sense it is "sometimes personified as a female deity." The Oxford lexicographers do not stop there but go on to recognize what they call a "strictly physical" sense, which is even lower in the moral scale: "the indulgence of the appetites, sensual gratification." The "unfavorable" significations of the word are dramatized by the English career of the most usual Latin word for pleasure, *voluptas*. Although some Latin-English dictionaries, especially those of the nineteenth century, say that *voluptas* means "pleasure, enjoyment, or delight of body or mind in a good or a bad sense," the word as it was used in antiquity seems to have been on the whole morally neutral and not necessarily intense. But the English words derived from *voluptas* are charged with moral judgment and are rather excited. We understand that it is not really to the minds of men that a voluptuous woman holds out the promise of pleasure, enjoyment, or delight. We do not expect a voluptuary to seek his pleasures in domesticity, or in the Imagination or Melancholy, or in smoking a pipe.

It is obvious that any badness or unfavorableness of meaning that the word pleasure may have relates to the primitiveness of the enjoyment that is being referred to. Scarcely any moralist will object to pleasure as what we may call a secondary state of feeling, as a charm or grace added to the solid business of life. What does arouse strong adverse judgment is pleasure in its radical aspect, as it is the object of an essential and definitive energy of man's nature. It was because Bentham's moral theory asserted that pleasure was indeed the object of an essential and definitive part of man's nature that Carlyle called it the Pig-philosophy. He meant, of course, that it impugned man's nature to associate it so immediately with pleasure. Yet this is just how Wordsworth asks us to conceive man's nature in the sentence I have spoken of—it is precisely pleasure in its primitive or radical aspect that he has in mind. He speaks of "the grand *elementary* principle of pleasure," which is to say, pleasure not as a mere charm or amenity but as the object of an instinct, of what Freud, whose complex exposition of the part that pleasure plays in life is of course much in point here, was later to call a *drive*. How little concerned was Wordsworth, at least in this one sentence, with pleasure in its mere secondary aspect is suggested by his speaking of it as constituting the *dignity* of man, not having in mind such dignity as is conferred by society but that which is *native* and *naked*.

When Carlyle denounced Bentham's assertion that pleasure

is, and must be, a first consideration of the human being, it was
exactly man's dignity that he was undertaking to defend. The
traditional morality to which Carlyle subscribed was certainly
under no illusion about the crude force of man's impulse to self-
gratification, but it did not associate man's dignity with this
force—on the contrary, dignity, so far as it was personal and
moral, was thought to derive from the resistance which man
offers to the impulse to pleasure.

For Wordsworth, however, pleasure was the defining attribute
of life itself and of nature itself—pleasure is the "impulse from
the vernal wood" which teaches us more of man and his moral
being "than all the sages can." And the fallen condition of
humanity—"what man has made of man"—is comprised by the
circumstance that man alone of natural beings does not experience
the pleasure which, Wordsworth believes, moves the living world.
It is of course a commonplace of Wordsworth criticism that, although the poet set the highest store by the idea of pleasure,
the actual pleasures he represents are of a quite limited kind.
Certainly he ruled out pleasures that are "strictly physical," those
which derive from "the indulgence of the appetites" and "sensual
gratification," more particularly erotic gratification. His living
world of springtime is far removed from that of Lucretius: nothing in it is driven by the irresistible power of *alma Venus*. This
is not to say that there is no erotic aspect to Wordsworth's mind;
but the eroticism is very highly sublimated—Wordsworth's pleasure always tended toward *joy,* a purer and more nearly transcendent state. And yet our awareness of this significant limitation
does not permit us to underrate the boldness of his statement in
the Preface about the primacy of pleasure and the dignity which

derives from the principle of pleasure, nor to ignore its intimate connection with certain radical aspects of the moral theory of the French Revolution.

For an understanding of the era of the Revolution, there is, I think, much to be gained from one of the works of the German economic historian, Werner Sombart, whose chief preoccupation was the origins of capitalism. In his extensive monograph, *Luxury and Capitalism,* Sombart develops the thesis that the first great accumulations of capital were achieved by the luxury trades in consequence of that ever-increasing demand for the pleasures of the world, for comfort, sumptuousness, and elegance, which is to be observed in Western Europe between the end of the Middle Ages and the end of the eighteenth century. As a comprehensive explanation of the rise of capitalism, this theory, I gather, has been largely discredited. Yet the social and cultural data which Sombart accumulates are in themselves very interesting, and they are much to our point.

Sombart advances the view that the European preoccupation with luxury took its rise in the princely courts and in the influence of women which court life made possible; he represents luxury as being essentially an expression of eroticism, as the effort to refine and complicate the sexual life, to enhance, as it were, the quality of erotic pleasure. The courtly luxury that Sombart studies is scarcely a unique instance of the association of pleasure with power, of pleasure being thought of as one of the signs of power and therefore to be made not merely manifest but conspicuous in the objects that constitute the *décor* of the lives of powerful men—surely Egypt, Cnossos, and Byzantium surpassed Renaissance Europe in elaborateness of luxury. But what would seem to be remarkable about the particular phenomenon that Sombart describes is the extent of its proliferation at a certain period— the sheer amount of luxury that got produced, its increasing availability to classes less than royal or noble, the overtness of desire for it, and the fierceness of this desire. Sombart's data on these points are too numerous to be adduced here, but any tourist, having in mind what he has even casually seen of the secondary arts of Europe from the centuries in question, the ornaments, furniture, and garniture of certain stations of life, will know that Sombart does not exaggerate about the amount of luxury produced. And any reader of Balzac will recognize the intensity of the passions which, at a somewhat later time, attended the acquisition of elaborate and costly objects which were desired as the means or signs of pleasure.

What chiefly engages our interest is the influence that luxury may be discovered to have upon social and moral ideas. Such an influence is to be observed in the growing tendency of power to express itself mediately, by signs or indices, rather than directly, by the exercise of force. The richness and elaboration of the objects in a princely establishment were the indices of a power which was actual enough, but they indicated an actual power which had no need to avow itself in action. What a prince conceived of as his dignity might, more than ever before, be expressed by affluence, by the means of pleasure made overt and conspicuous.

And as the objects of luxury became more widely available, so did the dignity which luxury was meant to imply. The connection between dignity and a luxurious style of life was at first not self-evident—in France in 1670 the very phrase *bourgeois gentilhomme* was thought to be comical. In the English translation of the title of Molière's comedy, *The Cit Turned Gentleman,* it was funny too, but the English laugh was neither so loud nor so long as the French. Tocqueville believed that it was the relatively easy growth of the English class of gentlemen, that is to say, the acceptance of the idea that the outward signs of status eventually conferred real status, which made an event like the Revolution of France unnecessary in England. Yet in France as in England, the downward spread of the idea of dignity, until it eventually became an idea that might be applied to man in general, was advanced by the increasing possibility of possessing the means or signs of pleasure. That idea, it need scarcely be said, established itself at the very heart of the radical thought of the eighteenth century. And Diderot himself, the most uncompromising of materialists, as he was the most subtle and delicate, could not have wanted a more categorical statement of his own moral and intellectual theory than Wordsworth's assertion that the grand elementary principle of pleasure constitutes the native and naked dignity of man, and that it is by this principle that man knows, and lives, and breathes, and moves.

Nothing so much connects Keats with Wordsworth as the extent of his conscious commitment to the principle of pleasure. But of course nothing so much separates Keats from his great master as his characteristic way of exemplifying the principle. In the degree that for Wordsworth pleasure is abstract and austere, for Keats it is explicit and voluptuous. No poet ever gave so much credence to the idea of pleasure in the sense of "indulgence of the appetites, sensual gratification," as Keats did, and the phenomenon that Sombart describes, the complex of pleasure-sensuality-luxury, makes the very fabric of his thought.

Keats's preoccupation with the creature-pleasures, as it manifests itself in his early work, is commonly regarded, even by some of his warmest admirers, with an amused disdain. At best it seems to derive from the kind of elegant minuscule imagination that used to design the charming erotic scenes for the lids of enameled sweetmeat and snuff boxes. At worst it seems to be downright vulgar in the explicitness of its concern with luxury. The word itself had a charm for Keats, and in his use of it he seems on the point of reviving its Middle English meaning, which is specifically erotic and nothing but erotic; for Chaucer, *luxures* were lusts and *luxurie* was licentiousness. Women present themselves to Keats's imagination as luxuries: "All that soft luxury/ that nestled in his arms." A poem is described as "a posy/ Of luxuries, bright, milky, soft and rosy." Poetry itself is defined by reference to objects of luxury, and even in its highest nobility, its function is said to be that of comforting and soothing.

Nor is the vulgarity—if we consent to call it that—confined to the early works; we find it in an extreme form in a poem of Keats's maturity. The lover in *Lamia* is generally taken to be an innocent youth, yet the most corrupt young man of Balzac's scenes of Parisian life would scarcely have spoken to his mistress or his fiancée as Lycius speaks to Lamia when he insists that she display her beauty in public for the enhancement of his prestige. Tocqueville said that envy was the characteristic emotion of plutocratic democracy, and it is envy of a particularly ugly kind that Lycius wishes to excite. "Let my foes choke," he says, "and my friends shout afar,/ While through the thronged streets your bridal car/ Wheels round its dazzling spokes." I am not sure that we should be at pains to insist that this is wholly a dramatic utterance and not a personal one, that we ought entirely to dissociate Keats from Lycius. I am inclined to think that we should suppose Keats to have been involved in all aspects of the principle of pleasure, even the ones that are vulgar and ugly. Otherwise we miss the full complication of that dialectic of pleasure which is the characteristic intellectual activity of Keats's poetry.

The movement of this dialectic is indicated in two lines from an early poem in which Keats speaks of "the pillowy silkiness that rests/ Full in the speculation of the stars"—it is the movement from the sensual to the transcendent, from pleasure to knowledge, and knowledge of an ultimate kind. Keats's intellect was brought into fullest play when the intensity of his affirmation of pleasure was met by the intensity of his skepticism about pleasure. The principle of pleasure is for Keats, as it is for Wordsworth, the principle of reality—by it, as Wordsworth said, we *know*. But for Keats it is also the principle of illusion. In *The Eve of St. Agnes,* to take the most obvious example, the moment of pleasure at the center of the poem, erotic pleasure expressed in the fullest possible imagination of the luxurious, is the very essence of reality: it is all we know on earth and all we need to know. And it is the more real as reality and it is the more comprehensive as knowledge exactly because in the poem it exists surrounded by what on earth denies it, by darkness, cold, and death, which make it transitory, which make the felt and proclaimed reality mere illusion.

But we must be aware that in Keats's dialectic of pleasure it is not only external circumstances that condition pleasure and bring it into question as the principle of reality, but also the very nature of pleasure itself. If for Keats erotic enjoyment is the peak and crown of all pleasures, it is also his prime instance of the way in which the desire for pleasure denies itself and produces the very opposite of itself.

> Love in a hut, with water and a crust,
> Is—Love, forgive us—cinders, ashes, dust;
> Love in a palace is perhaps at last
> More grievous torment than a hermit's fast.

This opening statement of the second part of *Lamia* is not, as it is often said to be, merely a rather disagreeable jaunty cynicism but one of Keats's boldest expressions of his sense that there is something perverse and self-negating in the erotic life, that it is quite in the course of nature that we should feel "Pleasure . . . turning to Poison as the bee-mouth sips." He insists on the seriousness of the statement in a way that should not be hard to interpret—referring to the lines I have just quoted, he says

> That is a doubtful tale from faery land,
> Hard for the non-elect to understand.

That faery land we know very well—in the Nightingale Ode, Keats's epithet for the region is *forlorn;* it is the country of La Belle Dame sans Merci, the scene of erotic pleasure which leads to devastation, of an erotic fulfillment which implies castration.

Keats, then, may be thought of as the poet who made the boldest affirmation of the principle of pleasure and also as the poet who brought the principle of pleasure into the greatest and *sincerest* doubt. He therefore has for us a peculiar cultural interest, for it would seem to be true that at some point in modern history the principle of pleasure came to be regarded with just such ambivalence.

This divided state of feeling may be expressed in terms of a breach between politics and art. Modern societies seek to fulfill themselves in affluence, which of course implies the possibility of pleasure. Our political morality is more than acquiescent to this intention. Its simple and on the whole efficient criterion is the extent to which affluence is distributed among individuals and nations. But another morality, that which we may describe as being associated with art, regards with a stern and even minatory gaze all that is implied by affluence, and it takes a dim or at best a very complicated view of the principle of pleasure. If we speak not only of the two different modes of morality, the political and the artistic, but also of the people who are responsive to them, we can say that it is quite within the bounds of possibility, if not of consistency, for the same person to respond, and intensely, to both of the two moral modes: it is by no means uncommon for an educated person to base his judgment of politics on a simple affirmation of the principle of pleasure, and to base his judgment of art, and also his judgment of personal existence, on a complex antagonism to that principle. This dichotomy makes one of the most significant circumstances of our cultural situation.

A way of testing what I have said about the modern artistic attitude to pleasure is afforded by the conception of poetry which Keats formulates in *Sleep and Poetry*. This poem does not express everything that Keats thought about the nature and function of poetry, but what it does express is undeniably central to his thought, and for the modern sensibility it is inadmissible and even repulsive. It tells us that poetry is gentle, soothing, cheerful, healthful, serene, smooth, regal; that the poet, in the natural course of his development, will first devote his art to the representation of the pleasures of appetite, of things that can be bitten and tasted, such as apples, strawberries, and the white shoulders of nymphs, and that he will give his attention to the details of erotic enticement amid grateful sights and odors, and to sexual fulfillment and sleep. The poem then goes on to say that, as the poet grows older, he will write a different kind of poetry, which is called nobler; this later kind of poetry is less derived from and directed to the sensuality of youth and is more fitted to the gravity of mature years, but it still ministers to pleasure and must therefore be strict in its avoidance of ugly themes; it must not deal with those distressing matters which are referred to as "the burrs and thorns of life"; the great end of poetry, we are told, is "to soothe the cares, and lift the thoughts of man."

Such doctrine from a great poet puzzles and embarrasses us. It is, we say, the essence of Philistinism.

The conception of the nature and function of poetry which Keats propounds is, of course, by no means unique with him—it can be understood as a statement of the common assumptions about art which prevailed through the Renaissance up to some point in the nineteenth century, when they began to lose their force.[1] Especially in the eighteenth century, art is closely asso-

---

[1] One of the last significant exponents of the old assumptions was the young Yeats. He was "in all things pre-Raphaelite"—a partisan, that is, not of the early and austere pre-Raphaelite mode, but of the later sump-

ciated with luxury—with the pleasure or at least the comfort of the consumer, or with the quite direct flattery of his ego. The very idea of Beauty seems to imply considerations of this sort, which is perhaps why the eighteenth century was so much drawn to the idea of the Sublime, for that word would seem to indicate a kind of success in art which could not be called Beauty because it lacked the smoothness and serenity (to take two attributes from Keats's catalogue) and the immediacy of gratification which the idea of Beauty seems to propose. But the Sublime itself of course served the purposes of egoism—thus, that instance of the Sublime which was called the Grand Style, as it is described by its great English exponent in painting, Sir Joshua Reynolds, is said to be concerned with "some instance of heroic action or heroic suffering" and its proper effect, Reynolds explains, is to produce the emotion which Bouchardon reported he felt when he read Homer: "His whole frame appeared to himself to be enlarged, and all nature which surrounded him diminished to atoms." [2]

---

tuous style, tinged with a sort of mystical eroticism—and he stubbornly resisted the realism of Carolus Duran and Bastien-Lepage, which was being brought back to England by the painters who had gone to study in Paris. His commitment to the "beautiful," as against truthful ugliness, was an issue of great moment between him and his father.

[2] All writers on the Sublime say in effect what Bouchardon says—that, although the sublime subject induces an overpowering emotion, even fear or terror, it does so in a way that permits us to rise superior to it and thus give us occasion to have a good opinion of our power of intellect and of ourselves generally. The Sublime has this direct relation to comfort and luxury, that it induces us "to regard as small those things of which we are wont to be solicitous" (Kant, *Critique of Aesthetic Judgment*). A more ambitious treatment of my subject would require a

In connection with the art of the eighteenth century I used the disagreeable modern word *consumer,* meaning thus to suggest the affinity that art was thought to have with luxury, its status as a commodity which is implied by the solicitude it felt for the pleasure and the comfort of the person who was to own and experience it. Certainly Wordsworth was preeminent in the movement to change this state of affairs,[3] yet Wordsworth locates the value of metrical language as lying in its ability to protect the reader from the discomfort of certain situations that poetry may wish to represent and he compares the effect of such situations in novels with their effect in Shakespeare, his point being that in novels they are "distressful" but in Shakespeare they are not.[4] It was, we know, an explanation which did not satisfy Keats, who was left to puzzle out why it is that in *King Lear* "all disagreeables evaporate." He discovers that this effect is achieved by "intensity," and we of our day are just at the point of being

much fuller exposition of the theory of the Sublime. Of this theory, which so much occupied the writers on art of the eighteenth century, it can be said that it has much more bearing upon our own literature than modern critics have recognized. The classic study in English is Samuel H. Monk's *The Sublime,* first published in 1935, now available as an Ann Arbor Paperback.

[3] ". . . Men . . . who talk of Poetry as a matter of amusement and idle pleasure; who will converse with us as gravely about a *taste* for Poetry, as they express it, as if it were a thing as indifferent as a taste for ropedancing, or Frontiniac, or Sherry."

[4] The strength of Wordsworth's impulse to suppress the "distressful" is suggested by the famous passage in *The Prelude* in which the poet explains how his childhood reading served to inure him to the terrors of actuality. He recounts the incident, which occurred when he was nine years old, of his seeing a drowned man brought up from the bottom of Esthwaite Lake. He was, he says, not overcome by fear of the "ghastly

comfortable with him when he disappoints our best hopes by
hedging: he is constrained to say that the "disagreeables" evaporate not only by the operation of intensity but also by "their
being in close connection with Beauty & Truth." But we do at
last find ourselves at one with him when, in his sonnet *On Sitting
Down to Read King Lear Once Again,* he dismisses all thought
of pleasure and prepares himself for the pain he is in duty bound
to undergo:

> . . . Once again, the fierce dispute
> Betwixt damnation and impassion'd clay
> Must I burn through; once more humbly assay
> The bitter-sweet of this Shakespearian fruit.

He is by no means certain that the disagreeables really will evaporate and that he will emerge whole and sound from the experience, and he prays to Shakespeare and "the clouds of Albion"
that they will guard him against wandering "in a barren dream,"
and that, when he is "consumed in the fire," they will contrive
his Phoenix-resurrection.

This we of our time can quite understand. We are repelled by
the idea of an art that is consumer-directed and comfortable, let
alone luxurious. Our typical experience of a work which will
eventually have authority with us is to begin our relation to it
at a conscious disadvantage, and to wrestle with until it consents

---

face," because his "inner eye" had seen such sights before in fairy tales
and romances. And then he feels it necessary to go further, to go beyond the bounds of our ready credence, for he tells us that from his reading
came "a spirit" which hallowed the awful sight

> With decoration and ideal grace
> A dignity, a smoothness, like the works
> Of Grecian Art, and purest poetry.

to bless us. We express our high esteem for such a work by sup-
posing that it judges us. And when it no longer does seem to
judge us, or when it no longer baffles and resists us, when we
begin to feel that we *possess* it, we discover that its power is
diminished. In our praise of it we are not likely to use the word
Beauty: we consented long ago—more than four decades ago—
to the demonstration made by I. A. Richards in collaboration with
Ogden and Wood that the concept of Beauty either could not
be assigned any real meaning, or that it was frivolously derived
from some assumed connection between works of art and our
sexual preferences, quite conventional sexual preferences at that.
"Beauty: it curves: curves are beauty," says Leopold Bloom, and
we smile at so outmoded an aesthetic—how like him! With a
similar amusement we read the language in which the young
Yeats praised beauty in *The Secret Rose* (1896)—he speaks of
those who are so fortunate as to be "heavy with the sleep/ Men
have named beauty." [5]

In short, our contemporary aesthetic culture does not set great

[5] Mr. Bloom's observation (which goes on to "shapely goddesses Venus,
Juno: curves the world admires" and "lovely forms of women sculped
Junonian") follows upon his lyrical recollection of his first sexual en-
counter with Molly; Yeats's phrase occurs in the course of a poem to
Maud Gonne. I think it is true to say of Joyce (at least up through
Ulysses) and of Yeats that they were among the last devotees of the
European cult of Woman, of a Female Principle which, in one way or
another, *ziegt uns hinein,* and that Molly and Maud are perhaps the last
women in literature to be represented as having a transcendent and on
the whole beneficent significance (although Lara in *Dr. Zhivago* should be
mentioned—it is she who gives that novel much of its archaic quality).
The radical change in our sexual mythos must surely be considered in
any speculation about the status of pleasure in our culture. It is to the
point, for example, that in Kafka's account of the spiritual life, which
is touched on below, women play a part that it at best ambiguous.

store by the principle of pleasure in its simple and primitive meaning and it may even be said to maintain an antagonism to the principle of pleasure. Such a statement of course has its aspect of absurdity, but in logic only. There is no psychic fact more available to our modern comprehension than that there are human impulses which, in one degree or another, and sometimes in the very highest degree, repudiate pleasure and seek gratification in—to use Freud's word—unpleasure.

The repudiation of pleasure in favor of the gratification which may be found in unpleasure is a leading theme of Dostoevsky's great *nouvelle, Notes from Underground.* Of this extraordinary work Thomas Mann has said that "its painful and scornful conclusions," its "radical frankness . . . ruthlessly transcending all novelistic and literary bounds" have "long become parts of our moral culture." Mann's statement is accurate but minimal— the painful and scornful conclusions of Dostoevsky's story have established themselves not only as parts of our moral culture but as its essence, at least so far as it makes itself explicit in literature.

Notes from Underground is an account, given in the first person, of the temperament and speculations of a miserable clerk, disadvantaged in every possible way, who responds to his un- fortunate plight by every device of bitterness and resentment, by hostility toward those of mankind who are more unfortunate than he is, and also by the fiercest contempt for his more fortunate fellow-beings, and for the elements of good fortune. He hates all men of purposeful life, and reasonable men, and action, and happiness, and what he refers to as "the sublime and the beauti- ful," and pleasure. His mind is subtle, complex, and contradictory almost beyond credibility—we never know where to have him and in our exhaustion we are likely to explain his perversity in some simple way, such as that he hates because he is envious, that he despises what he cannot have: all quite natural. But we are not permitted to lay this flattering unction to our souls— for one thing, he himself beats us to that explanation. And although it is quite true, it is only a small part of the truth. It is also true that he does not have because he does not wish to have; he has arranged his own misery—arranged it in the interests of his dignity, which is to say, of his freedom. For to want what is commonly thought to be appropriate to men, to want whatever it is, high or low, that is believed to yield pleasure, to be active about securing it, to use common sense and prudence to the end of gaining it, this is to admit and consent to the *conditioned* nature of man. What a distance we have come in the six decades since Wordsworth wrote his Preface! To know and feel and live and move at the behest of the principle of pleasure—this, for the Underground Man, so far from constituting his native and naked dignity, constitutes his humiliation in bondage. It makes him, he believes, a mechanic thing, the puppet of whoever or whatever can offer him the means of pleasure. If pleasure is indeed the principle of his being, he is as *known* as the sum of 2 and 2; he is a mere object of reason, of that rationality of the Revolution which is established upon the primacy of the principle of pleasure.

At one point in his narrative, the protagonist of *Notes from Underground* speaks of himself as an "anti-hero." He is the eponymous ancestor of a now-numerous tribe. He stands as the antagonistic opposite to all the qualities which are represented by that statue of Sophocles which Professor Margarete Bieber

tells us we are to have in mind when we try to understand the
Greek conception of the hero, the grave beauty of the countenance
and physique expressing the strength and order of the soul; the
Underground Man traces his line of descent back to Thersites.
It is in his character of anti-hero that he addresses the "gentlemen," as he calls them, the men of action and reason, the lovers
of the "sublime and the beautiful," and brags to them, "I have
more life in me than you have."

More life: perhaps it was this boast of the Underground Man
that Nietzsche recalled when he said, "Dostoevsky's Underman
and my Overman are the same person clawing his way out of
the pit [of modern thought and feeling] into the sunlight." One
understands what Nietzsche meant, but he is mistaken in the
identification, for his own imagination is bounded on one side
by that word *sunlight,* by the Mediterranean world which he
loved: by the tradition of humanism with its recognition of the
value of pleasure. He is ineluctably constrained by considerations
of society and culture, however much he may despise his own
society and culture, but the Underground Man is not. To be
sure, the terms of the latter's experience are, in the first instance,
social; he is preoccupied by questions of status and dignity, and
he could not, we may suppose, have come into existence if the
fates of the heroes of Balzac and Stendhal had not previously
demonstrated that no object of desire or of the social will is anything but an illusion and a source of corruption, society being
what it is. But it is the essence of the Underground Man's position that his antagonism to society arises not in response to the
deficiencies of social life, but, rather, in response to the insult
society offers his freedom by aspiring to be beneficent, to embody

"the sublime and the beautiful" as elements of its being. The anger Dostoevsky expresses in *Notes from Underground* was mobilized not by the bad social condition of Russia in 1864 but by the avowed hope of some people that a good social condition could be brought into being. A Utopian novel of the day, Chernyshevsky's *What Is to Be Done?*, represented to him a particularly repugnant expression of this hope.[6] His disgust was aroused by this novel's assumption, that man would be better for a rationally organized society, by which was meant, of course, a society organized in the service of pleasure. Dostoevsky's reprobation of this idea, begun in *Notes from Underground*, reached its climax in Ivan Karamazov's poem of The Grand Inquisitor, in which again, but this time without the brilliant perversities of the earlier work, the disgust with the specious good of pleasure is the ground for the affirmation of spiritual freedom.

I have taken the phrase "specious good" from a passage in

[6] "A Utopian novel of the day" does not, of course, give anything like an adequate notion of the book's importance in the political culture of Russia. Dostoevsky chose his antagonist with the precision that was characteristic of him, for Chernyshevsky, who thought of himself as the heir of the French Enlightenment, by his one novel exercised a decisive influence upon the Russian revolutionaries of the next two generations, most notably upon Lenin, who borrowed its title for one of his best-known pamphlets and whose moral style was much influenced by the character Rakhmétov. This paragon of revolutionists, although very fond of the luxury in which he was reared, embraces an extreme asceticism because, as he says, "We demand that men may have a complete enjoyment of their lives, and we must show by our example that we demand it, not to satisfy our personal passions, but for mankind in general; that what we say we say from principle and not from passion, from conviction and not from personal desire." Only one pleasure is proof against Rakhmétov's iron will—he cannot overcome his love of expensive cigars.

Wallace Fowlie's little book on Rimbaud, in which Mr. Fowlie discusses what he calls "the modern seizure and comprehension of spirituality." Without evasion, Mr. Fowlie identifies a chief characteristic of our culture which critics must inevitably be conscious of and yet don't like to name. If we are to be aware of the spiritual intention of modern literature, we have to get rid of certain nineteenth-century connotations of the word spiritual, all that they may imply to us of an overrefined and even effeminate quality, and have chiefly in mind what Mr. Fowlie refers to when he speaks of a certain type of saint and a certain type of poet and says of them that "both the saint and the poet exist through some propagation of destructive violence." And Mr. Fowlie continues: "In order to discover what is the center of themselves, the saint has to destroy the world of evil, and the poet has to destroy the world of specious good."

The destruction of what is considered to be specious good is surely one of the chief literary enterprises of our age. Whenever in modern literature we find violence, whether of represented act or of expression, and the insistence upon the sordid and the disgusting, and the insult offered to the prevailing morality or habit of life, we may assume that we are in the presence of the intention to destroy specious good, that we are being confronted by that spirituality, or the aspiration toward it, which subsists upon violence against the specious good.

The most immediate specious good that a modern writer will seek to destroy is, of course, the habits, manners, and "values" of the bourgeois world, and not merely because these associate themselves with much that is bad, such as vulgarity, or the exploitation of the disadvantaged, but for other reasons as well, because they clog and hamper the movement of the individual spirit toward freedom, because they prevent the attainment of "more life." The particular systems and modes of thought of the bourgeois world are a natural first target for the modern spirituality. But it is not hard to believe that the impulse to destroy specious good would be as readily directed against the most benign society, which, by modern definition, serves the principle of pleasure.

In the characteristically modern conception of the spiritual life, the influence of Dostoevsky is definitive. By comparison with it, the influence of Nietzsche is marginal. For however radical Nietzsche was in criticism of the existing culture, the terms of his adversity were, as I have remarked, essentially social and humanistic. The moral and personal qualities suggested by a particular class, the aristocracy, had great simple force with him and proposed to his imagination a particular style of life. Despite the scorn he expressed for liberal democracy and socialist theory as he knew them, he was able to speak with sympathy of future democracies and possible socialisms, led to do so by that element of his thought which served to aerate his mind and keep it frank and generous—his awareness of the part played in human existence by the will to power, which, however it figures in the thought of his epigones and vulgarizers, was conceived by Nietzsche himself as comprising the whole range of the possibilities of human energy, creativity, libido. The claims of any social group to this human characteristic had weight with him. And he gave ready credence to the pleasure that attends one or another kind of power; if he was quick to judge people by the pleasures they chose—and woe to those who preferred beer to wine and *Parsifal* to *Carmen!*—the principle of pleasure presented itself to

him as constituting an element of the dignity of man. It is because of this humanism of his, this naturalistic acceptance of
power and pleasure, that Nietzsche is held at a distance by the
modern spiritual sensibility. And the converse of what explains
Nietzsche's relative marginality explains Dostoevsky's position
at the very heart of the modern spiritual life.

If we speak of spirituality, we must note that it is not only
humanism that is negated by the Underground Man but Christianity as well, or at least Christianity as Western Europe understands it. For not only humanism but the Christianity of the
West bases reason upon pleasure, upon pleasure postponed and
purified but analogous in kind to worldly pleasure. Dostoevsky's
clerk has had his way with us: it would seem to be true that, in
the degree that the promises of the spiritual life are made in
terms of pleasure—of comfort, rest, and beauty—they have no
power over the modern imagination. If Kafka, perhaps more
than any other writer of our time, lends the color of reality to
the events of the spiritual life, his power to do so lies in his
characterizing these events by unpleasure, by sordidness and
disorder, even when, as in *The Castle,* the spiritual struggle
seems to yield a measure of success. He understood that a
divinity who, like St. Augustine's, could be spoken of as gratify-
ing all the senses, must nowadays be deficient in reality, that a
heaven which is presented to us as well ordered, commodious,
beautiful—as *luxurious*—cannot be an object of hope. He was
set on the road to this understanding by Dostoevsky, who, more
dramatically and cogently than anyone before him, expresses the
modern aversion from pleasure. Yeats tells us that "Berkeley in
his youth described the summum bonum and the reality of
Heaven as physical pleasure, and thought this conception made

both more intelligible to simple men." To simple men perhaps, but who now is a simple man? How far from our imagination is the idea of "peace" as the crown of spiritual struggle! The idea of "bliss" is even further removed. The two words propose to us a state of virtually infantile passivity which is the negation of the "more life" that we crave, the "more life" of spiritual militancy. We dread Eden, and of all Christian concepts there is none which we understand so well as the *felix culpa* and the "fortunate fall"; not, of course, for the reason on which these Christian paradoxes were based, but because by means of the sin and the fall we managed to get ourselves expelled from that dreadful place.

I have tried to make explicit, although surely in a way that is all too summary, a change in the assumptions of literature which everybody is more or less aware of. In undertaking to do this, my first intention has been historical and objective. But it must be obvious that my account of the change has not been wholly objective in the sense of being wholly neutral. It asks a question which is inevitably adversary in some degree, if only by reason of the irony which is implicit in the historical approach to a fact of moral culture. It suggests that the modern spirituality, with its devaluation of the principle of pleasure, because it came into being at a particular time, may be regarded as a contingent and not a necessary mode of thought. This opens the way to regarding it as a mode of thought which is "received" or "established" and which is therefore, like any other received or established mode of thought, available to critical scrutiny.

And that possibility is by no means comfortable. We set great

store by the unillusioned militancy of spirit which deals violently with the specious good. Upon it we base whatever self-
esteem we can lay claim to—it gives us, as one of D. H. Lawrence's characters says of it (or something very much like it),
our "last distinction"; he feels that to question it is a "sort of
vulgarity." [7] To what end, with what intention, is it to be questioned? Can an adversary scrutiny of it point away from it to
anything else than an idiot literature, to "positive heroes" who
know how to get the good out of life and who have "affirmative"
emotions about their success in doing so? The energy, the consciousness, and the wit of modern literature derive from its enterprise of violence against the specious good of whatever poor
"pleasure" may be offered to us by the universe or by our general
culture in its quotidian aspects. We feel an instinctive resentment
of questions which tend to suggest that there is fault to be found
with the one saving element of our moral situation—that extruded "high" segment of our general culture, with its exigent,
violently subversive spirituality, with its power of arming us
against, and setting us apart from, all in the general culture that
we hate and fear.

Then what justification can there be for describing with any
irony at all the diminished status of the principle of pleasure
which characterizes this segment of our culture?

Possibly one small justification can be brought to light by
reference to a famous passage in the *Confessions* of St. Augustine, the one in which Augustine speaks of an episode of his
adolescence and asks why he entered that orchard and stole
those pears. Of all the acts of his unregenerate days which he

[7] Gerald Crich, in Chapter XXIX of *Women in Love*.

calls sinful and examines in his grim, brilliant way, there is none that he nags so persistently, none that seems to lie so far beyond the reach of his ready comprehension of sin. He did not steal the pears because he was hungry. He did not steal them because they were delicious—they were pears of rather poor quality, he had better at home. He did not steal them to win the admiration of the friends who were with him, although this comes close, for, as he says, he would not have stolen them if he had been alone. In all sin, he says, there is a patent motivating desire, some good to be gained, some pleasure for the sake of which the act was committed. But this sin of the stolen pears is, as it were, pure—he can discover no human reason for it. He speaks again of the presence of the companions, but although their being with him was a necessary condition of the act, it cannot be said to have motivated it. To the mature Augustine, the petty theft of his youth is horrifying not only because it seems to have been a sin committed solely for the sake of sinning, but because, in having no conceivable pleasure in view, it was a sort of negative transcendence—in effect, a negation—of his humanity. This is not strange to us—what I have called the high extruded segment of our general culture has for some time been engaged in an experiment in the negative transcendence of the human, a condition which is to be achieved by freeing the self from its thralldom to pleasure. Augustine's puzzling sin is the paradigm of the modern spiritual enterprise, and in his reprobation of it is to be found the reason why Dostoevsky contemned and hated the Christianity of the West, which he denounced as, in effect, a vulgar humanism.

To be aware of this undertaking of negative transcendence is,

surely, to admire the energy of its desperateness. And we can
comprehend how, for the consumer of literature, for that highly
developed person who must perforce live the bourgeois life in
an affluent society, an aesthetic ethos based on the devaluation of
pleasure can serve, and seem to save, one of the two souls which
inhabit his breast. Nearly overcome as we are by the specious
good, insulted as we are by being forced to acquire it, we claim
the right of the Underground Man to address the "gentlemen"
with our assertion, "I have more life in me than you have,"
which consorts better with the refinement of our sensibility than
other brags that men have made, such as, "I am stronger than
you," or "I am holier than thou." Our high culture invites us to
transfer our energies from the bourgeois competition to the
spiritual competition. We find our "distinction"—last or penul-
timate—in our triumph over the miserable "gentlemen," whether
they are others or ourselves, whether our cry be, "I have more
life in me than you have" or "I have more life in me than I
have." Now and then it must occur to us that the life of competition for spiritual status is not without its sordidness and absurdity. But how else are we to live?

But this is a matter for the novelist—for that novelist we do
not yet have but must surely have one day, who will take into
serious and comic account the actualities of the spiritual career of
our time.

More immediately available to our awareness and more sub-
stantive and simple in itself is the effect which the devaluation
of pleasure has upon the relation between our high literature
and our life in politics, taking that word in its largest possible
sense. There was a time when literature assumed that the best

ideals of politics were naturally in accord with its own essence, when poetry celebrated the qualities of social life which had their paradigmatic existence in poetry itself. Keats's *Poems* of 1817 takes for its epigraph two lines from Spenser which are intended to point up the political overtone of the volume: "What more felicity can fall to creature/ Than to enjoy delight with liberty." Even when Wordsworth is deep in Toryism and Stoic Christianity, it is natural for him to assert the Utopian possibility.

> Paradise and groves
> Elysian, Fortunate Fields—like those of old
> Sought in the Atlantic Main—why should they be
> A history only of departed things,
> Or a mere fiction of what never was?

He goes on to say categorically that these imaginations may become, at the behest of rationality and good will, "a simple produce of the common day." But the old connection between literature and politics has been dissolved. For the typical modern literary personality, political life is likely to exist only as it makes an occasion for the disgust and rage which are essential to the state of modern spirituality, as one particular instance of the irrational, violent, and obscene fantasy which life in general is, as licensing the counter-fantasy of the poet.

In a recent essay,[8] William Phillips described in an accurate and telling way the dichotomy that has developed between modern literature and a rational and positive politics, and went on to explain why, for literature's sake, the separation must be maintained. "It now looks," Mr. Phillips said,

[8] "What Happened in the 30's," *Commentary,* September, 1962.

as though a radical literature and a radical politics must be kept apart. For radical politics of the modern variety has really served as an antidote to literature. The moral hygiene, the puritanism, the benevolence—all the virtues that sprout on the left—work like a cure for the perverse and morbid idealism of the modern writer. If writing is to be thought of as radical, it must be in a deeper sense, in the sense not simply of cutting across the grain of contemporary life but also of reaching for the connections between the real and the forbidden and the fantastic. The classic example is Dostoevsky.

The situation that Mr. Phillips describes will scarcely be a matter of indifference to those of us who, while responding to the force of the perverse and morbid idealism of modern literature, are habituated to think of literature and politics as naturally having affinity with each other. We cannot but feel a discomfort of mind at the idea of their hostile separation, and we are led to ask whether the breach is as complete as Mr. Phillips says it is. His description, it seems to me, so far as it bears upon the situation of the moment, upon the situation as it presents itself to the practitioner of literature, needs no modification. But if we consider the matter in a more extended perspective, in the long view of the cultural historian, it must occur to us to speculate—even at the risk of being "hygienic"—whether the perverse and morbid idealism of modern literature is not to be thought of as being precisely political, whether it does not express a demand which in its own way is rational and positive and which may have to be taken into eventual account by a rational and positive politics.

If we do ask this question, we will be ready to remind ourselves that the devaluation of the pleasure principle, or, as perhaps we ought to put it, the imagination of going *beyond the pleasure principle* is, after all, not merely an event of a particular moment in culture. It is, as Freud made plain in his famous essay, a fact of the psychic life itself. The impulse to go beyond the pleasure principle is certainly to be observed not only in modern literature but in all literature, and of course not only in literature but in the emotional economy of at least some persons in all epochs. But what we can indeed call an event in culture is that at a particular moment in history, in our moment, this fact of the psychic life became a salient and dominant theme in literature, and also that it has been made explicit as a fact in the psychic life and forced upon our consciousness by Freud's momentous foray into metapsychology. And this cultural event may indeed be understood in political terms, as likely to have eventual political consequences, just as we understood in political terms and as having had political consequences the eighteenth-century assertion that the dignity of man was to be found in the principle of pleasure.

We deal with a change in quantity. It has always been true of some men that to pleasure they have preferred what the world called unpleasure. They imposed upon themselves difficult and painful tasks, they committed themselves to strange, "unnatural" modes of life, they sought out distressing emotions, in order to know psychic energies which are not to be summoned up in felicity. These psychic energies, even when they are experienced in self-destruction, are a means of self-definition and self-affirmation. As such, they have a social reference—the election of unpleasure, however isolate and private the act may be, must refer to society if only because the choice denies the valuation which society in general puts upon pleasure; and of course it often receives social approbation in the highest degree, even if at a remove of time: it is the choice of the hero, the saint and martyr, and, in some cultures, the artist. The quantitative change which we have to take account of is: what was once a mode of experience of a few has now become an ideal of experience of many. For reasons which, at least here, must defy speculation, the ideal of pleasure has exhausted itself, almost as if it had been actually realized and had issued in satiety and ennui. In its place, or, at least, beside it, there is developing—conceivably at the behest of literature!—an ideal of the experience of those psychic energies which are linked with unpleasure and which are directed toward self-definition and self-affirmation. Such an ideal makes a demand upon society for its satisfaction: it is a political fact.

What I have called the spirituality of modern literature can scarcely be immune from irony, and the less so as we see it advancing in the easy comprehension of increasing numbers of people, to the point of its becoming, through the medium of the stage and the cinema, the stuff of popular entertainment—how can irony be withheld from an accredited subversiveness, an established moral radicalism, a respectable violence, an entertaining spirituality? But although the anomalies of the culture of the educated middle class do indeed justify an adversary response, and perhaps a weightier one than that of irony, yet a response that is nothing but adversary will not be adequate.

We often hear it said nowadays, usually by psychoanalysts and by writers oriented toward psychoanalysis, that the very existence of civilization is threatened unless society can give credence to the principle of pleasure and learn how to implement it. We understand what is meant, that repressiveness and oppression will be lessened if the principle of pleasure is established in our social arrangements, and we readily assent. Yet secretly we know that the formula does not satisfy the condition it addresses itself to—it leaves out of account those psychic energies which press beyond the pleasure principle and even deny it.

It is possible to say that—whether for good or for bad—we confront a mutation in culture by which an old established proportion between the pleasure-seeking instincts and the ego instincts is being altered in favor of the latter.[9] If we follow

[9] I said something to this effect when, in "On the Modern Element of Modern Literature" (*Partisan Review,* January–February, 1961), I commented on the status of tragedy in our culture. I ventured the opinion that the tragic mode is not available to us—this was not, I said, a mark of our spiritual inferiority—because we do not think of the degradation or downfall of the protagonist as a deplorable event: what he loses in the worldly way we judge to be well lost for the sake of the reality and truth, the ultimate self-realization, which we understand tragedy to bring. I based my generalization on our response to the fate of Kurtz in *Heart of Darkness* and Aschenbach in *Death in Venice.* Lionel Abel, in the brilliant chapter on tragedy in his *Metatheatre,* says that a tragedy—a real tragedy, of which Mr. Abel believes there are only a very few—must have for its protagonist a "daemon," that is to say, a person who, "having lived through tragic destruction . . . becomes divine, a daemon." I understand Mr. Abel to be saying that the tragic destruction is the extirpation of "merely" human feelings, that the daemonic existence comes with the protagonist's survival of the death of the pleasure-seeking instincts. Kurtz and Aschenbach become daemons, or nearly, but our emotions don't take into account the "destruction" or fall as the traditional emotions in response to tragedy were supposed to do.

For a full and detailed account of the modern devaluation of that good fortune the destruction of which once pained us in tragedy, see

Freud through the awesome paradoxes of *Beyond the Pleasure Principle,* we may understand why the indications of this change should present themselves as perverse and morbid, for the other name that Freud uses for the ego instincts is the death instincts. Freud's having made the ego instincts synonymous with the death instincts accounts, more than anything else in his dark and difficult essay, for the cloud of misunderstanding in which it exists. But before we conclude that *Beyond the Pleasure Principle* issues, as many believe, in an ultimate pessimism or "negation," and before we conclude that the tendencies in our literature which we have remarked on are nothing but perverse and morbid, let us recall that although Freud did indeed say that "the aim of all life is death," the course of his argument leads him to the statement that "the organism wishes to die only in its own fashion," only through the complex fullness of its appropriate life.

Thomas Munro, "The Failure Story: A Study of Contemporary Pessimism," *The Journal of Aesthetics and Art Criticism,* Vol. XVII, No. 2, December, 1958.

René Wellek

ROMANTICISM RE-EXAMINED

IN A long paper, "The Concept of Romanticism in Literary History," published in the first two numbers of the newly founded journal, *Comparative Literature* (1949),[1] I tried to refute the thesis propounded by A. O. Lovejoy that the term "Romantic" means nothing, that "the 'Romanticism' of one country may have little in common with that of another," and that "the romantic ideas were in large part heterogeneous, logically independent, and sometimes essentially antithetic to one another in their implications."[2] I was distressed at the general acceptance of Lovejoy's thesis by the American academic community: scholars had given up such questions in despair and settled down to an investigation of facts and the interpretation of individual poems. I felt that Lovejoy's extreme nominalism encouraged shirking the larger issues of literary history: the concepts of period, movement, development, and the whole question of the unity and diversity of European cultural change. Lovejoy, an eminent his-

[1] *Comparative Literature*, I (1949), 1–23, 147–72.
[2] "On the Discrimination of Romanticisms," *PMLA*, XXIX (1924), 229–53, reprinted in *Essays in the History of Ideas* (Baltimore, 1948), pp. 228–53; and "The Meaning of Romanticism for the Historian of Ideas," *Journal of the History of Ideas*, II (1941), 261.

torian of ideas, paradoxically contributed to the antihistorical
drift of recent American literary scholarship. In that article I
traced the history of the terms "Romantic" and "Romanticism"
in order to show the large measure of agreement about their
meaning during the age in all countries. I collected evidence which
proved that even without the use of the terms the consciousness
of a specific change was universal at that time, and finally, I
tried to demonstrate, in a very empirical way, that the poetry of
the early nineteenth century has many features in common: the
new views of nature, imagination, and the use of symbol are all-
pervasive in Europe, and they are, *pace* Lovejoy, obviously coherent and mutually implicate each other.

Lovejoy has not defended his thesis, but he has reasserted it:
in the preface to a little book, *The Reason, the Understanding
and Time* (1961),[3] which analyzes some ideas of Schelling, Jacobi,
Schopenhauer, and Bergson, Lovejoy reprints the crucial passages
of his earlier essays in order to justify his avoidance of calling
these philosophers "Romantic." Ronald S. Crane, whom I had
quoted dismissing "the fairy tales about neo-classicism and romanticism in the 18th century," [4] commented at some length on
my article: he did not object to historical generalizations which
would describe the change in the terms I had selected, but he
considered my "passion for unity" excessive. He demanded "literal
proof": he wanted me to show "sameness in the literal sense" of
the terms of "imagination," "nature," and "symbol" in all the
writers discussed.[5] Crane has set me an impossible task: I do not

[3] Baltimore, 1961. Preface.
[4] *Philological Quarterly*, XXII (1943), 143.
[5] In *Philological Quarterly*, XXIX (1950), 257–59.

see how anybody can prove a literal identity exclusive of all individuality. This would imply a monolithic period such as could not be found at any time in history. In all my writings I have consistently argued for a period concept which allows for the survival of former ages and the anticipations of later ones. "Period" demands the dominance (but not the total tight dictatorial rule) of a set of norms which, in the case of Romanticism, are provided sufficiently by similar or analogous concepts of the imagination, nature, symbol, and myth. I am content with Crane's admission of such generalizations, and I grant that Lovejoy, in *The Great Chain of Being* and in some later papers, actually operates with concepts such as "organicism, dynamism, and diversitarianism" which are descriptive of what usually is called "Romantic." The mere avoidance of the term in Lovejoy's new book on Schelling and his followers solves nothing.

Morse Peckham, in a widely noted article, "Toward a Theory of Romanticism" (1951),[6] wanted, he says, "to reconcile Lovejoy and Wellek, and Lovejoy with himself" by singling out the criterion of "organic dynamism" as the definition of Romanticism. Peckham thus accepts the concept of nature and imagination as described in my article, but drops the concern for symbol and myth. Peckham introduces a new concept, "negative romanticism," that is, despairing, nihilistic romanticism. The argument runs that positive romanticism does not fit Byron, but that "negative romanticism" does. I am supposed to be unable "to come to terms" with this phenomenon. Still, it seems to me that little has been accomplished by calling familiar states of mind— *Weltschmerz, mal du siècle,* pessimism—"negative" romanticism.

[6] In *PMLA*, LXI (1951), 5–23.

It is a purely verbal solution: as if we should call naturalism "negative symbolism," or symbolism "negative naturalism." By showing the coherence of the point of view which other writers as well as I have called "Romanticism"—its organicism, its use of the creative imagination, its symbolic and mythic procedures —we have excluded nihilism, "alienation" from our definition. A man who considers nature dead and inimical to man, who considers imagination merely a combinatory associative power, and who does not use symbolic and mythic devices is not a Romanticist in the sense in which Wordsworth, Novalis, and Hugo are Romantic.

Since the 1951 article Morse Peckham has changed his mind. In a new essay, "Toward a Theory of Romanticism. Reconsiderations" (1961),[7] Peckham abandons his early scheme in favor of a grandiose cultural history of the modern age, which he has also developed in a book, *Beyond the Tragic Vision* (1962).[8] Peckham now calls Romanticism Enlightenment, as he has been apparently deeply impressed by Ernest Tuveson's *The Imagination as a Means of Grace: Locke and the Aesthetics of Romanticism* (1960).[9] But Tuveson, though excellent on Lockean influences on eighteenth-century British aesthetics, cannot show that imagination was considered a "means of grace" at that time. In any case, the break with the Lockean tradition is precisely a crucial test of Romantic aesthetics. I need only allude to Coleridge's rejection of Locke or to Schelling's view of Locke's "bestialities" reported by Henry Crabb Robinson.[10] Be that as it

---

[7] In *Studies in Romanticism,* I (1961), 1–8.
[8] New York, 1962.   [9] Berkeley, Calif., 1960.
[10] Coleridge's views of Locke are collected in Roberta F. Brinkley,

may, Peckham now believes the essence of Romanticism to be the imposition of order on chaos: a heroic antimetaphysical subjectivism which reminds one rather of Bertrand Russell's "A Free Man's Worship" than of the outlook of a Wordsworth, a Friedrich Schlegel, or a Lamartine. Peckham takes a quite unjustified view of Kant as a kind of pragmatist. "Romanticism learns from Kant," he says, "that it can do entirely without constitutive metaphysics and can use any metaphysic or world hypothesis as supreme fiction." I am not aware of a single writer in the late eighteenth or the early nineteenth century to whom this description would apply. Who then rejected the possibility of metaphysics or treated it as supreme fiction? Not even Friedrich Schlegel, whose theory of irony exposed him to the charge of "probabilism," opportunism, and aestheticism. I am afraid Peckham's "reconsiderations" do not contribute to a better definition of "Romanticism": it seems only right that he avoids the term in *Beyond the Tragic Vision.*

Reading Peckham, one is tempted to give up the problem in despair. We might come to agree with Lovejoy or even with Valéry, who warns us that it "is impossible to think seriously with words such as Classicism, Romanticism, Humanism, or Realism. One cannot get drunk or quench one's thirst with labels on a bottle." [11] But of course these terms are not labels: they

---

Coleridge on the Seventeenth Century (Durham, N.C., 1955), pp. 67–109. For Schelling on Locke, see *H. C. Robinson in Germany,* ed. E. Morley (Oxford, 1929), p. 118. Letter dated Nov. 14, 1802.

[11] *Mauvaises pensées* (Paris, 1942), p. 35: "Il est impossible de penser sérieusement avec les mots comme Classicisme, Romantisme, Humanisme, Réalisme. On ne s'enivre ni ne se désaltère avec des étiquettes de bouteille."

have a range of meaning very different from Pabst Blue Ribbon or Liebfrauenmilch. Modern logicians tell us that all definitions are verbal, that they are "stipulated" by the speaker. We certainly cannot prevent Communists from calling dictatorship "popular democracy," a baby from calling any strange man "daddy," or even Peckham from calling romanticism "Enlightenment." But "there is a sense"—I am quoting Wilbur Urban—"in which the distinction between verbal and real definition is a valid one. There comes a point at which variation ceases to be merely inconvenient and unpragmatic; it becomes unintelligible. It leads to *contradictio in adjecto,* in which intrinsic incompatibility between subject and predicate destroys the meaning by an implicit denial." [12] We can dismiss people who speak of "square circles" or call Romanticism Enlightenment. We need not even consider our task identical with that of the lexicographer, who has to document the full range of usage of a term. We shall rather try to show that there is a growing area of agreement and even convergence among the definitions or, more modestly, descriptions of Romanticism as they have been attempted by responsible scholars in recent decades in several countries. Incidentally, I hope, the survey will bring out the differences in methods and approaches characteristic of literary scholarship in Germany, France, England, and the United States. But precisely the varieties of national traditions which are often only in tenuous contact with each other will make the basic consensus about the nature of Romanticism stand out all the more convincingly.

In Germany in the early twenties, a whole series of books was devoted specifically to definitions of the nature or essence of Ro-

[12] *The Intelligible World* (New York, 1929), p. 124.

manticism. Germans operate, or rather operated, with dichoto-
mies, thesis and antithesis, vast contrasts such as idea and form,
idea and experience, rationalism and irrationalism, perfection and
infinitude, etc. Max Deutschbein, in *Das Wesen des Romantischen*
(1921),[13] aims at a phenomenological intuition of the essence of
Romanticism by showing the agreement between English and
German Romanticism in their concept and use of the synthetic
imagination: the union of opposites, the finite and infinite, eternity and temporality, universality and individuality. The scheme
serves the conclusion that English poetry translated German
theory into practice, but, of course, the amazing identities which
Deutschbein finds between German and English Romanticism
are often due to the fact that his crown witness on the English
side, Coleridge, is simply paraphrasing Schelling. Still, this neglected little book has stressed one central and valid concept: the
reconciling, synthetic imagination as the common denominator
of Romanticism.

The scheme of contrasts elaborated by Fritz Strich in *Deutsche
Klassik und Romantik: Oder Vollendung und Unendlichkeit*
(1922) [14] has a different starting point. Strich wants to transfer
Wölfflin's *Kunstgeschichtliche Grundbegriffe* (1915) to the history
of literature. Wölfflin ingeniously contrasted Renaissance and
Baroque art on purely structural grounds such as "open" or
"closed" form. Strich ties the contrast between classical and Romantic art rather to man's quest for permanence or eternity.[15]

---

[13] Coethen, 1921.   [14] Munich, 1922.

[15] Strich seems to have elaborated a suggestion from Heine's *Romantische
Schule* (1833). See *Sämtliche Werke,* ed. O. Walzel, VII (Leipzig, 1910),
14. "Die klassische Kunst hatte nur das Endliche darzustellen, und ihre

Eternity can be achieved either in perfection or in infinitude. The history of man oscillates between these two poles. "Perfection wants repose. Infinitude: movement and change. Perfection is closed, infinitude open. Perfection is clear, the Infinite is dark. Perfection seeks the image, infinitude the symbol." [16] The transfer of Wölfflin's categories from art-history to literature is accomplished ingeniously, but one wonders whether the description of Romanticism as dynamic, open form, unclear, symbolic, and the like does more than line up Romanticism with the Baroque and with Symbolism in the series of polar alternations between intellect and feeling which are supposed to constitute the history of Europe. It is the old separation into sheep and goats: a schematic device which obscures the historical particularities of the Romantic age in distinction from other open-form, dynamic, symbolic styles. Still, Strich and his many followers have been extraordinarily successful in bringing out these very broad changes in feelings and art-forms which were hardly perceived before Wölfflin and others devised the vocabulary for their description.

The whole enterprise is apparently still a novelty in the United States: thus the philosopher W. T. Jones, in his new book, *The Romantic Syndrome* (1961),[17] makes the most extravagant claims

---

Gestalten konnten identisch sein mit der Idee des Künstlers. Die romantische Kunst hatte das Unendliche und lauter spiritualistische Beziehungen darzustellen oder vielmehr anzudeuten, und sie nahm ihre Zuflucht zu einem System traditioneller Symbole oder vielmehr zum Parabolischen."

[16] Strich, *Deutsche Klassik und Romantik,* pp. 7–8: "Vollendung ist unwandelbare Ruhe. Unendlichkeit: Bewegung und Verwandlung. Vollendung ist geschlossen, Unendlichkeit aber offen. Vollendet ist die Einheit. . . . Vollendet ist die Klarheit, unendlich aber das Dunkel. . . . Vollendet also ist das Bild, unendlich aber das Sinnbild."

[17] The Hague, 1961.

for his discovery of a scheme which is very similar to that of many Germans. According to Jones, Romanticism is dynamic rather than static, prefers disorder to order, continuity to discreteness, soft focus to sharp focus, has an inner rather than an outer bias, and prefers an other world to this world.[18] Jones seems unaware of the many typologies of this kind in Germany. The names of Dilthey, Spranger, Jaspers, Jung, and Nohl do not occur anywhere in the book.[19] The only theory known to Jones seems to be Wölfflin's, to whom he refers in a footnote. Wölfflin's categories, Jones admits, "seem related to my axes," but Jones thinks that it is his discovery that "these categories permit a cross-medium comparison between artistic productions and literary and philosophical works."[20] Jones's analysis of art works, of the contrast between Dürer and Rubens, Bellini and El Greco, is completely dependent on Wölfflin. The application to Romantic poetry, which interests us here, never gets beyond the simplest observations. Romantic poetry prefers the misty, the hazy, the dim, the soft-focus (Wölfflin's "unclearness"). Inner bias is illustrated easily, so is preference for disorder, love of continuity, the other world, etc. Most of these are familiar themes, and Jones's examples seem often ill chosen. He uses, for instance, quotations from Goethe's *Faust* without heeding the dramatic context.[21] Jones's main con-

[18] Jones, *The Romantic Syndrome*, p. 118.

[19] See Wilhelm Dilthey, "Die Typen der Weltanschauung" (1911), in *Gesammelte Schriften* (Leipzig, 1931), VIII, 75–118; Eduard Spranger, *Lebensformen* (Halle, 1914); Karl Jaspers, *Psychologie der Weltanschauungen* (Berlin, 1919); C. G. Jung, *Psychologische Typen* (Zurich, 1921); Herman Nohl, *Stil und Weltanschauung* (Jena, 1923).

[20] Jones, *The Romantic Syndrome*, p. 48.

[21] For example, Faust's speech answering Margaret's question about his belief: "Wer darf ihn nennen? . . . ." must not be interpreted as a pro-

tribution to typology is the ominous suggestion that it needs verification by quantification: the idea that a team of researchers should, for instance, make a count of soft-focus imagery in all the poems published in a given year. Jones imagines that by such statistical methods it would be possible to give an objective date for the rise of Romanticism.[22] I shall not urge the difficulties and uncertainties of this enterprise: the impossibility of establishing criteria for what is soft-focus in imagery and for defining an image, and of counting the images in every poem in all languages. One must rather reject the whole ideal of knowledge implied: the fashionable faith in statistics, the denial of the crucial issue of value and individuality.

The many German definitions of Romanticism were surveyed by Julius Petersen, in *Die Wesensbestimmung der deutschen Romantik* (1926).[23] Petersen welcomed each and every approach, including the racial, which makes Romanticism peculiarly German, and the regional, which makes it East German in particular. But at the time of his writing the tide was beginning to turn. More and more reservations against the whole method were being voiced both inside and outside of Germany. Martin Schütze, a Professor of German at the University of Chicago, made in his *Academic Illusions* (1933)—a neglected book now happily again available in a reprint [24]—trenchant criticisms of the whole German phantasmagoria of polarities. Emil Staiger, just before

fession of Goethe's faith as Jones assumes (p. 131). Faust tries to avoid a clear answer.

[22] Jones, *The Romantic Syndrome,* pp. 227 ff.   [23] Leipzig, 1926.

[24] Chicago, 1933. New ed., Hamden, Conn., 1962, with Preface by René Wellek.

the outbreak of the Second World War, announced in the preface to *Die Zeit als Einbildungskraft des Dichters* (1939) that the task of literary study is "interpretation," and he dismissed influences, biography, psychology, sociology, and typology from the inner sanctum.[25] In his late years at Harvard Karl Vietor voiced his conviction that "the age of the *geistesgeschichtlich* approach and its methods is at an end." [26]

As far as I can ascertain, only two new German books about the nature of Romanticism have appeared since the end of the war. Adolf Grimme, in *Vom Wesen der Romantik* (1947),[27] defined Romanticism as a breakthrough of what he calls "the vegetative strata of the soul": the preconscious rather than the subconscious. The preconscious includes the imagination, which is raised to consciousness by Romanticism. Grimme is more interesting in his theoretical defense of the method of phenomenology. A single example, he argues, must suffice, as we cannot deduce or generalize about Romanticism before we know what is meant by Romanticism. The aim of a verbal definition is illusory: we can only point to what is romantic as we can point to the color red. In a collection of lectures, *Romantik* (1948), the well-known Jesuit philosopher Romano Guardini comes to a similar conclusion: Romanticism is "an upsurge of the unconscious and primitive." [28]

[25] Zurich, 1939. "Einleitung: Von der Aufgabe und den Gegenständen der Literaturwissenschaft."

[26] "Deutsche Literaturgeschichte als Geistesgeschichte," *PMLA*, LX (1945), 899–916. P. 914: "Die Epoche der geisteswissenschaftlichen Betrachtungsweise und ihrer Methoden ist offenbar abgeschlossen."

[27] Braunschweig, 1947.

[28] "Erscheinung und Wesen der Romantik," in *Romantik: Ein Zyklus*

The comparisons with English Romanticism made in Germany have become very cautious. Horst Oppel, in an article, "Englische und deutsche Romantik" (1956),[29] makes much of the differences between the two countries: the prevalence of an empirical philosophy in England, the uniqueness of the German fairy tale, the rarity of romantic irony in England, and so forth. A British professor of German writing in German, Eudo C. Mason, has recently elaborated on this theme in *Deutsche und englische Romantik* (1959).[30] He rightly emphasizes the very different historical situation of the English Romantic poets, who were not confronted with such overpowering figures as those of Goethe and Schiller in Germany. He points to features in German Romanticism such as a nihilistic daring, satanism, decadentism, and extreme aestheticism which go far beyond the bourgeois limitations of Wordsworth or Coleridge. Mason makes much of the almost complete lack of understanding and contacts between the two countries. To my mind he overemphasizes the timidity, orthodoxy, and prudery of the English poets. He plays up the role of Henry Crabb Robinson as the only person of the time who understood both Wordsworth and the German Romantics, though he must admit that Robinson was historically quite ineffective and that his published articles hardly reflect the presumed depth of his understanding. Robinson's attempt, in 1829, to convert

Tübinger Vorlesungen, ed. Theodor Steinbüchel (Tübingen, 1948), pp. 237-49.

[29] In *Die Neueren Sprachen,* Heft 10 (1956), pp. 457-75. Reprinted in *The Sacred River: Studien und Interpretationen zur Dichtung der englischen Romantik* (Frankfurt, 1959), pp. 5-24.

[30] Göttingen, 1959.

Goethe to Wordsworth by recruiting Ottilie von Goethe was pitifully inept. There was, one must conclude, no real meeting of minds (though a few physical encounters) between Coleridge and Tieck, or Coleridge and August Wilhelm Schlegel. But surely the problem of the affinity between German and English Romanticism cannot be disposed of by showing that contemporary contacts were tenuous and personal sympathies far from perfect.

There is, of course, plenty of reasearch and interpretation in Germany of individual Romantic writers, but on the whole a strange silence has settled around the question of the nature or essence of Romanticism.

In France the situation is very different. Paul Van Tieghem attempted a synthesis of all European Romantic literatures in *Le Romantisme dans la littérature européenne* (1948).[31] Van Tieghem aims at writing literary history on a truly international scale: he draws liberally also from the small European literatures, including the Slavic and Scandinavian. He deliberately ignores national frontiers and orders his facts not according to a linguistic atlas but by a psychological and aesthetic map of tendencies and tastes. Categories such as "the feeling for nature," "religion," "love," "exoticism," "historicism" assemble a mass of information, but unfortunately never rise to any higher level of generalization. Oddly enough, Van Tieghem can say that "the suppression of the mythological style is probably the most universal trait of formal romanticism." [32] Van Tieghem, though learned and

[31] Vol. 76 of *L'Evolution de l'humanité*, ed. Henri Beer (Paris, 1948).
[32] *Ibid.*, p. 14: "La suppression de ce style mythologique conventionele est peut-être le caractère le plus universel du romantisme formel."

acutely aware of the unity of Europe, lacks the *esprit de finesse* and remains disconcertingly external.[33] An examination of recent definitions of Romanticism by Jean-Bertrand Barrère lists nothing new.[34] He prefers to engage in a discussion of the different stages of French Romanticism: a historical task which is not our concern.

Much more exciting and original are the studies of the group of critics who call themselves critics of consciousness or the Geneva school. They seem to live in a world quite different from that of the older academic scholars. Albert Béguin's *L'Âme romantique et le rêve* (1939)[35] studies German Romanticism and the French writers who, in his opinion, went the same way, Rousseau, Sénancour, Nodier, Maurice de Guérin, Hugo, Nerval; he glances at Baudelaire, Rimbaud, Mallarmé, and Proust. Béguin is not particularly concerned with influences: his motivation is ultimately religious. "The greatness of romanticism" resides for him in "its having recognized and affirmed the profound resemblance of poetic states and the revelations of a religious order."[36] But Béguin is also a scholar interested in defining the essence of Romanticism. Romanticism is to him a myth: man

[33] A similar book is Giovanni Laini's *Il Romanticismo europeo* (2 vols.; Florence, 1959), wide-ranging but purely external. It begins with anti-classical polemics in the fifteenth century and ends with present-day Romanticism.

[34] "Sur quelques Définitions du romantisme," in *Revue des sciences humaines,* Fsc. 62–63 (1959), pp. 93–110.

[35] Marseille, 1939. I quote the new ed., Paris, 1946, in one volume, which unfortunately drops the critical apparatus and the bibliography.

[36] *L'Ame romantique et le rêve,* p. 401: "La grandeur de romantisme restera d'avoir reconnu et affirmé la profonde ressemblance des états poétiques et des révélations d'ordre religieux."

invents myths in order to overcome his solitude and to reintegrate himself into the whole. He invents myths in a double sense: he finds them in the treasure-house of history and discovers them in dreams and the unconscious. Béguin distinguishes three Romantic myths: those of the soul, of the unconscious, and of poetry. Poetry is the only answer to the elemental anguish of the creature enclosed in his temporal existence. The analogical concept of the universe is assumed: the structure of our mind and our total being and its spontaneous rhythms are identical with the structure and the great rhythms of the universe.[37] Béguin's horizon is confined to German and French literature. He focuses on the German theorists, speculative philosophers, and doctors of the unconscious, and studies sympathetically such writers as Jean Paul, Novalis, Brentano, Arnim, and E. T. A. Hoffmann. A student of English Romanticism might conclude that he singles out the most irrationalistic writers and isolates the dream, the night, the unconscious unduly, but I believe that even for a parallel study of English developments, we would find in Béguin the finest understanding of the nature of the Romantic imagination and its rootedness in a sense of the continuity between man and nature and the presence of God.

Georges Poulet, in his books and articles mainly concerned with the feeling of time and space, supports Béguin's conclusions by a somewhat different method. The early books, *Etudes sur le temps humain* and *La Distance intérieure* (1950, 1952), are both devoted to individual French writers, though the appendix to the English translation of *Studies in Human Time* contains thumbnail sketches of American writers from Emerson to Henry

[37] *Ibid.*, pp. 395-96, 400-1.

James and T. S. Eliot.[38] But in an article, "Timelessness and Romanticism" (1954),[39] and in a section, "Le Romantisme," of the
new book, *Les Métamorphoses du cercle* (1961),[40] Poulet generalizes about Romanticism boldly. The article in the *Journal
of the History of Ideas* tries to define the specific experience of
time common to many Romantics: to Rousseau, Coleridge, De
Quincey, Baudelaire. They all seem to have experienced param-
nesia, the sensation of *déjà vu,* the total recollection which does
not appear to be recollected; they all aimed, at least, at the total
exclusion of the past from the present by a perfect absorption
in the present, as if time stood still and became eternity. But
Poulet rightly emphasizes that this Romantic experience is not
identical with its philosophical source: the Neoplatonic "simultaneous and perfect possession of an interminable life." The Romantics did not want to describe an ideal world or the abstract
existence of God in their poems. They wanted to express their
own concrete experiences, their own personal apprehension of
human timelessness. "In brief, paradoxically, they brought Eternity into Time." [41] In the new book, Poulet defines Romanticism
in somewhat different terms: as a consciousness of the funda-
mentally subjective nature of the mind, as a withdrawal from
reality to the center of the self, which serves as starting point
for a return to nature. Poulet draws his examples of this back-
and-forth movement of the mind mainly from French writers,
but also from Coleridge and Shelley, quoting and using in-

[38] Paris, 1950 and 1952. *Studies in Human Time,* translated by Elliott
Coleman (Baltimore, 1956).

[39] In *Journal of the History of Ideas,* XV (1954), 3–22.

[40] Paris, 1961.   [41] *Journal of the History of Ideas,* XV (1954), 7.

geniously but overinsistently the figures of the circle and circumference. Shelley's saying that "poetry is at once the centre
and the circumference of knowledge" pleases him as much as
Coleridge's admiring an old coach-wheel. "See how the rays pro-
ceed from the centre to the circumference, and how many different
images are distinctly comprehended at one glance, as forming
one whole, and each part in some harmonious relation to each
and all." The wheel is the symbol of beauty, of organic wholeness, of the unity of the universe.[42]

Poulet's conception of criticism had originally excluded the
possibility of such generalizations about a period: each author,
according to Poulet, lives in his particular world construed by
his own "consciousness." The task of the critic is to enter this
individual consciousness.[43] But apparently Poulet now conceives
of these consciousnesses as unified in an all-embracing spirit of the
time: he boldly generalizes about the Renaissance, the Baroque,
and Romanticism. Romanticism—not only French or German but
all Romanticism—is defined by this effort to overcome the opposition of subject and object, of center and circumference, in a
personal experience.

The same view is advanced by Albert Gérard, in *L'Idée romantique de la poésie en Angleterre* (1955),[44] and summarized

[42] Quoted in *Métamorphoses du cercle*, p. 148, from *The Defence of
Poetry*, and on p. 155 from Coleridge, *Miscellanies Aesthetic and Literary*
(London, 1911), p. 20.

[43] For a trenchant criticism of Poulet's method see Leo Spitzer, "A
propos de la Vie de Marianne," in *Romanische Literaturstudien* (Tübingen,
1959), pp. 248–76, and my review in *The Yale Review*, XLVI (1956),
114–19.

[44] Paris, 1955.

in an article, "On the Logic of Romanticism" (1957).[45] Gérard also rejects as inadequate the older generalizations about Romanticism: its emotionalism, cult of spontaneity, primitivism, and the like, and he examines minutely, by traditional methods, the views common to Wordsworth, Coleridge, Shelley, and Keats (Byron is expressly excluded) of the poetic experience as a form of knowledge, an intuition of cosmic unity conceived as a matter-spirit continuum. The philosophy of creativity, the union of subject and object, the role of the symbol and myth are expounded by Gérard with ample documentation. The results will strike us as not particularly new. Gérard brings, however, welcome corroboration to recent students of romantic theory. I need only allude to Meyer Abrams's *The Mirror and the Lamp* (1953) [46] and to the second volume of my *History of Modern Criticism* (1955).[47] Abrams emphasizes the shift from imitation theory to theory of expression, from the mirror to the lamp: or rather, from the mechanistic metaphorical analogies of neoclassical theory to the biological imagery of the Romanticists. He pays some attention to the German background of English theories. In my own book I give a full exposition of the Germans and distinguish between a Romantic movement in a wider sense, as a revolt against neoclassicism, and a Romantic movement in a more special sense, as the establishment of a dialectical and symbolist view of poetry. It thus seems a firmly established fact that there was a coherent Romantic theory of poetry which has been defined and analyzed.

[45] In *Essays in Criticism*, VII (1957), 262–73.
[46] New York, 1953. Cf. my review in *Comparative Literature*, VI (1954), 178–81.
[47] Vol. II: *The Romantic Age* (New Haven, 1955).

Poetic theory implies a philosophical attitude and a poetic practice, certainly, in the Romantic age. An agreement on the basic outlook of the Romantics on reality and nature and on the main devices used by the Romantic poets has also been reached among recent English and American students. What matters in a study of poetry is the function of the Romantic view of nature. "The Structure of Romantic Nature Imagery" (1949) was explored by W. K. Wimsatt: he shows how the metaphor organizes a Romantic nature poem, how, e.g., the landscape in Coleridge's sonnet "To the River Otter" is "both the occasion of reminiscence and the source of the metaphors by which reminiscence is described," how the Romantic poems blur the distinction between literal and figurative because the poet wants to read a meaning into the landscape, but also wants to find it there.[48] Meyer H. Abrams, in "The Correspondent Breeze: A Romantic Metaphor" (1957), shows how this recurrent image represents "the chief theme of continuity and interchange between outer motions and interior life and powers" in many important Romantic poems, such as Coleridge's *Dejection: An Ode* and Wordsworth's *Prelude*.[49] Abrams refuses to be drawn into inferences about archetypal patterns: he argues that this mode of reading eliminates the individuality of a poem, and threatens to nullify even its status as a work of art. Several other sensitive studies, mostly concerned with Wordsworth, have recently led to the same conclusion: e.g., Geoffrey Hartman's

[48] In *The Verbal Icon: Studies in the Meaning of Poetry* (Lexington, Ky., 1954), pp. 103–16. The quotation is on p. 109.

[49] In *The Kenyon Review*, XIX (1957), 113–30. Quoted from reprint in *English Romantic Poets: Modern Essays in Criticism*, ed. M. H. Abrams (New York, 1960), pp. 37–54. Quotation on p. 39.

paper "A Poet's Progress: Wordsworth and the *Via naturaliter negativa*" (1962) describes how Nature itself led the poet beyond nature. But the Nature is not Nature as such, but Nature indistinguishably blended with Imagination or, as Hartman formulates it paradoxically, "the Imagination experienced as a power distinct from Nature opens the poet's eyes by putting them out." [50] Another writer, Paul de Man, in a paper entitled "Symbolic Landscape in Wordsworth and Yeats" (1962), describes this double vision which allows Wordsworth to see landscapes as "objects as well as entrance gates to a world lying beyond visible nature." Wordsworth's transcendental vision is contrasted with Yeats's emblematic landscape.[51] David Ferry, in *The Limits of Mortality: An Essay on Wordsworth's Major Poems* (1959), seems to overstate Wordsworth's hatred for the mortal limitations of man: he misconceives his mood, I believe. But he sees that nature is, in Wordsworth, a "metaphor for eternity, for the absence of death," that "the theory of symbolism posits as its ground the double consciousness . . . whereby the objects of nature may have individual and particular identity in themselves as objects, yet will stand 'figuratively' for the whole of which they really are part." [52] In Earl Wasserman's turgid and forced interpretations, both in the book on Keats, called *The Finer Tone* (1953), and in the more recent *The Subtler Language* (1959), we find this awareness that the poetic act is creative both of a cosmic system and of the poem made possible by that

[50] In *Modern Philology*, LIX (1962), 214–24. Quotation on p. 224.

[51] In *In Defense of Reading*, ed. Reuben A. Brower and Richard Poirier (New York, 1962), pp. 22–37. Quotation on p. 28.

[52] Middletown, Conn., 1959. Quotations on pp. 16, 37.

system. Wasserman hardly overstates Romantic individualism when he says that "the creation of a poem is also the creation of the cosmic wholeness that gives meaning to the poem, and each poet must independently make his own world-picture, his own language within language." [53] This ambition justifies the Romantic concern for symbolism and mythology, and for a symbolism and mythology which is individual and private, relies on personal vision, and hence is open to the most diverse and often contradictory interpretations. The most influential study of Romantic key images and myths was G. Wilson Knight's *Starlit Dome* (1941).[54] We all have learned from Wilson Knight: I suspect that even Georges Poulet has read him with profit. His spatial approach, the way of seeing "a poem or a play at once in a single view, like a patterned carpet," [55] has become the model of many later readings. But most of us have become increasingly dissatisfied with the arbitrariness of his associations, the intrusion of a crude psychoanalysis and of a strangely misused Nietzsche. Few of us can share the odd exaltation of Byron to a symbolist and prophet, to the greatest man after Christ. But in the chapter "The Wordsworthian Profundity" Knight comes to the right conclusion that Wordsworth aims at a "fusion of mind with nature to create the living paradise," to which, however, in Knight's opinion, Shelley and Keats "bear stronger *immediate* witness" than Wordsworth.[56] Knight's themes have been pursued

[53] Baltimore, 1953 and 1959. The quotation from *The Subtler Language,* p. 186.

[54] *Starlit Dome: Studies in the Poetry of Vision* (Oxford, 1941; new ed., London, 1959).

[55] *Ibid.,* p. xii, from Introduction by W. F. Jackson Knight.

[56] *Ibid.,* p. 82.

by others, often with a different emphasis: W. H. Auden's *The Enchafèd Flood: The Romantic Iconography of the Sea* (1950) centers on the longing for the sea from Wordsworth to Mallarmé, with emphasis on *Moby Dick*. Auden sees a dialectic of consciousness and unconsciousness: "Romanticism means the identification of consciousness and sin: the Romanticist yearns for innocence because he is" traveling farther and farther from "unconsciousness." [57] In the introduction to the fourth volume of *Poets of the English Language* (1950), Auden states the same conclusion somewhat differently: as self-consciousness is the noblest human quality, the artist as the most conscious man becomes the Romantic hero. But "the idol of consciousness is a pantheistic god immanent in nature." [58] In the same year, F. W. Bateson concluded that "the nature-symbol, the synthetic link between the conscious and the subconscious mind, is the basic unit of Romantic poetry." [59] Also R. A. Foakes's *The Romantic Assertion* (1958) describes the Romantic system of symbols as serving the "vision of harmony." In a rather obvious way this Romantic "vocabulary of assertion" is contrasted with the modern poetry of conflict and irony.[60] On the other hand, Frank Kermode, in his *Romantic Image* (1957), derives the modern symbol, mainly in Yeats, directly from Romanticism. "The Symbol of the French is the Romantic Image writ large and given more elaborate metaphysical and magical support." But Kermode considers Symbolism a "great and in some ways noxious historical

[57] New York, 1950, p. 150.
[58] Ed. W. H. Auden and Norman Holmes Pearson (New York, 1950), pp. xv–xvi.
[59] In *English Poetry: A Critical Introduction* (London, 1950), p. 126.
[60] London, 1958, pp. 50, 182.

myth," and wants to destroy the idea of the supernatural image and what he considers its inevitable accompaniment: the alienated artist, the artist as a pretentious prophet and seer.[61]

An opposite and emphatically positive evaluation of Romantic mythology is made in Harold Bloom's *The Visionary Company* (1961), a book which interprets closely all the main Romantic poems with less polemical fervor than his earlier work on *Shelley's Mythmaking* (1959).[62] Bloom exalts Blake and Shelley. Their vision is interpreted as gnostic rapture transcending that of the more nature-bound Wordsworth and Keats. I find many of Bloom's readings totally unconvincing. Thus, he invokes Blake's inept picture of the Tiger—"a shabby pawn-shop sort of stuffed tiger, more an overgrown house-cat"—to misread the whole poem as a mockery revealing "a state of being beyond either Innocence or Experience, a state where the lamb can lie down with the tiger." [63] Nor are Wordsworth or Keats interpreted rightly: Bloom minimizes both the Christian and the Hellenic constituents of Romanticism. He sees only the prophetic, the visionary of the company.[64] We shall not, I think, make much progress with the problem of Romanticism if we seek its prototype in such an exceptional and lonely figure as Blake, who seems to me rather a survival from another century, however much he may also anticipate the issues of our own time.

What is called Romanticism in England and on the Continent is not the literal vision of the mystics but the concern for the reconciliation of subject and object, man and nature, conscious-

[61] London, 1957, pp. 5, 166.   [62] New Haven, 1959.

[63] Garden City, N.Y., 1961, p. 31.

[64] Cf. the review by Paul de Man in *The Massachusetts Review,* III (1962), 618–23.

ness and unconsciousness to which we have returned several times. It is well brought out in two recent studies which deal with both English and Continental Romanticism. E. D. Hirsch, in *Wordsworth and Schelling* (1960),[65] defines the convergence of these strikingly different figures in a whole spectrum of ideas: the way of reconciling time and eternity, the immanent theism, the dialectic which favors what Hirsch calls "both/and thinking," the fear of alienation, the concept of living nature, and the role of the imagination which makes explicit the implicit unity of all things. Hirsch construes a typology which he derives from Karl Jaspers's *Psychologie der Weltanschauungen* (1919), and thus he avoids the question of common sources and influences. Surely, however, we must assume that the Neoplatonic tradition and the nature mysticism of Jakob Boehme translated into eighteenth-century terms lie behind both Wordsworth and Coleridge, as well as Schelling.

Paul de Man, in an article, "Structure intentionelle de l'image romantique" (1960),[66] redefines the nature of the Romantic nature image. He uses passages about the high Swiss mountains from Rousseau, Wordsworth, and Hölderlin to show the peculiar paradox of the Romantic poet's nostalgia for the object. Language strives to become nature. The words must, in a phrase of Hölderlin's, "arise like flowers" (*wie Blumen entstehn*). "Sometimes romantic thought and poetry seem about to surrender so completely to the nostalgia for the object that it becomes difficult to distinguish between object and image, between imagination and perception, between expressive and constitutive language

[65] New Haven, 1960.
[66] *Revue internationale de philosophie,* XIV (1960), 68–84, esp. 74–75, 83.

and mimetic and literal language." De Man thinks of passages in Wordsworth and Goethe, Baudelaire and Rimbaud where the "vision becomes almost a presence, a real landscape." But he argues that even the most extreme believer in the magic of language, Mallarmé, never doubted the intrinsic ontological primacy of the natural and earthly object. But the attempt of language to approach the ontological status of the object fails. Contradicting his statement a few pages before, De Man concludes that we have misunderstood these poets if we call them "pantheists" while "they are probably the first writers who, within the Western Hellenic and Christian tradition, have in their poetic language questioned the ontological primacy of the sensible object." Though De Man seems to waver on the issue of the Romantics' precise view of nature, he strongly corroborates our central theme. The reconciliation of art and nature, language and reality is the Romantic ambition.

In a recent essay, "Romanticism and 'Antiself-Consciousness'" (1962), Geoffrey Hartman has generalized about the common elements in English and German Romanticism. The peculiarly Romantic remedy for the human predicament is the attempt "to draw the antidote to self-consciousness from consciousness itself." The idea of a return to nature or naiveté via knowledge is common to German and English Romanticism. He concludes that "to explore the transition from self-consciousness to imagination, and achieve that transition while exploring it is the most crucial Romantic concern." The modern writer, while pursuing the same aim, has lost faith in the role of nature.[67]

In all of these studies, however diverse in method and em-

[67] In *The Centennial Review*, VI (1962), 553-65.

phasis, a convincing agreement has been reached: they all see the implication of imagination, symbol, myth, and organic nature, and see it as part of the great endeavor to overcome the split between subject and object, the self and the world, the conscious and the unconscious. This is the central creed of the great Romantic poets in England, Germany, and France. It is a closely coherent body of thought and feeling. We can, of course, still insist that there is also a unity of Romanticism on the lowest literary level: in the Renascence of Wonder, in the Gothic romance, in the interest in folklore and in the Middle Ages. H. H. Remak, in a paper, "West-European Romanticism: Definition and Scope" (1961), has recently drawn up a large synoptic table where he lists many criteria proposed and answers "yes" or "no" whether they apply to Germany, France, England, Italy, or Spain. He comes to the welcome conclusion that "the evidence pointing to the existence in Western Europe of a widespread, distinct and fairly simultaneous pattern of thought, attitudes and beliefs associated with the connotation 'Romanticism' is overwhelming," [68] though Italy and Spain were the countries least affected by Romanticism. But his tables have the drawback of being atomistic: the implication and coherence of the concepts of nature, imagination, and myth are not shown, and such old criteria as "liberalism" or "vagueness," and such ideas as "rhetoric" or "greater positive emphasis on religion" are given an undeserved status.

I dislike being called "the champion of the concept of a pan-

[68] In *Comparative Literature: Method and Perspective,* ed. Newton P. Stallknecht and Horst Frenz (Carbondale, Ill., 1961), pp. 223–59.

European Romanticism." [69] I would not be understood as mini-
mizing or ignoring national differences or forgetting that great
artists have created something unique and individual. Still, I
hope to have shown that in recent decades a stabilization of
opinion has been achieved. One could even say (if we did not
suspect the word so much) that progress has been made not
only in defining the common features of Romanticism but in
bringing out what is its peculiarity or even its essence and nature:
that attempt, apparently doomed to failure and abandoned by
our time, to identify subject and object, to reconcile man and
nature, consciousness and unconsciousness by poetry which is
"the first and last of all knowledge." [70]

[69] *Ibid.*, p. 227.
[70] Preface to the second edition of *Lyrical Ballads* (1800). In *Poetical
Works,* ed. E. de Selincourt (Oxford, 1944), II, 396.

SUPERVISING COMMITTEE,

THE ENGLISH INSTITUTE, 1962

Richard Ellmann (*1962*), CHAIRMAN, NORTHWESTERN UNIVERSITY

Clara Marburg Kirk (*1962*), DOUGLASS COLLEGE

Howard M. Schless (*1962*), COLUMBIA UNIVERSITY

Warner Rice (*1963*), UNIVERSITY OF MICHIGAN

William Nelson (*1963*), COLUMBIA UNIVERSITY

Eugene Waith (*1963*), YALE UNIVERSITY

Jean Hagstrum (*1964*), NORTHWESTERN UNIVERSITY

George Ford (*1964*), UNIVERSITY OF ROCHESTER

Grace Calder (*1964*), HUNTER COLLEGE

Harold C. Martin, SECRETARY, HARVARD UNIVERSITY

THE PROGRAM

SEPTEMBER 4 THROUGH SEPTEMBER 7, 1962

Conferences

I. A RECONSIDERATION OF ROMANTICISM
Directed by Northrop Frye, Victoria College, Toronto
   1. THE DRUNKEN BOAT: THE REVOLUTIONARY ELEMENT IN ROMAN-
      TICISM
      Northrop Frye, Victoria College, Toronto
   2. ENGLISH ROMANTICISM: THE SPIRIT OF THE AGE
      M. H. Abrams, Cornell University
   3. WORDSWORTH TO DOSTOEVSKY: THE FATE OF PLEASURE
      Lionel Trilling, Columbia University
   4. THE UNITY OF EUROPEAN ROMANTICISM
      René Wellek, Yale University

II. TRAVEL LITERATURE

   Directed by Warner G. Rice, University of Michigan
   1. THE ROMANTIC TRANSFORMATION OF TRAVEL LITERATURE
      George B. Parks, Queens College
   2. TRAVEL LITERATURE AND THE RISE OF NEO-HELLENISM IN ENG-
      LAND
      James M. Osborn, Yale University

3. MANKIND AT A DISTANCE: THE INVERTING TELESCOPE OF THE
   COSMIC VOYAGE
   Mark R. Hillegas, University of Michigan

4. THE ROAD TO REALITY: BURLESQUE TRAVEL LITERATURE AND
   MARK TWAIN'S *Roughing It*
   Franklin R. Rogers, University of Wisconsin at Milwaukee

III. AUDEN

Directed by Monroe K. Spears, University of the South

1. THE POEM AS PERFORMANCE
   John G. Blair, Michigan State University at Oakland

2. AUDEN AS CRITIC
   Cleanth Brooks, Yale University

3. WORDS FOR MUSIC
   Monroe K. Spears, University of the South

IV. IDEAS IN LITERATURE: THE DRAMA

*Directed by Vivian Mercier, City College, City University of
New York*

1. THE GREEK DRAMA OF IDEAS
   William Arrowsmith, University of Texas

2. FROM MYTH TO IDEAS—AND BACK
   Vivian Mercier, City College, City University of New York

3. THE DANGER OF IDEAS
   Denis Johnston, Smith College

EVENING MEETING, SEPTEMBER 6

Mr. David Lloyd, NEW YORK CITY CENTER OPERA
Wolfgang Schanzer, Accompanist
*A Program of Love Songs (English, French, German, Italian,
Russian, American)*

Kenneth T. Abrams, Queens College; M. H. Abrams, Cornell University; Ruth M. Adams, Douglass College, Rutgers; Gellert S. Alleman, Rutgers State University; Marcia Allentuck, C.C.N.Y.; Reta Anderson, Emory University; Mother Mary Anthony, Rosemont College; Jane Appelbe, Waterloo University College (Canada); Joseph Appleyard, s.j., Harvard University; George Arms, University of New Mexico; Robert Ayers, Georgetown University; George Bahlke, Middlebury College; Ashur Baizer, Ithaca College; J. M. Barnard, Yale University; R. A. Barrell, Monash University (Australia); Mary P. Barrows, University of California; Sister Marie of the Trinity Barry, Emmanuel College; Phyllis Bartlett, Queens College; F. W. Bateson, Corpus Christi, Oxford (England); Mrs. F. W. Bateson; Lester A. Beaurline, University of Virginia; David W. Becker, Miami University; Karl Beckson, Brooklyn College; Alice R. Bensen, Eastern Michigan University; Lienhard Bergel, Queens College; Sister Rose Bernard, c.s.j., College of St. Rose; Walter Bezanson, Rutgers State University; William O. Binkley, University of Virginia; John C. Blair, Michigan State University (Oakland); Whitney Blake, Oxford University Press; Haskell Block, Brooklyn College; Philip Bordinat, Miami University; Sister Mary Charlotte Borthwick, F.C.S.P., Providence Heights College; C. Francis Bowers, F.S.C., Manhattan College;

John D. Boyd, s.j., Fordham University; Robert Bradford, Lafayette College; Sister Mary Brian, Rosary College; Mary Campbell Brill, Madison College; Paul Brodtkorb, University of Connecticut; Cleanth Brooks, Yale University; Reuben Brower, Harvard University; Nancy Bryant, Emma Willard School; C. O. Burgess, Old Dominion College; Bro. Fidelian Burke, La Salle College; Katherine Burton, Wheaton College; Jess Byrd, Salem College; Grace Calder, Hunter College; Edward Callahan, College of the Holy Cross; Edward Callan, Western Michigan University; Kenneth Neill Cameron, Carl H. Pforzheimer Library; Sister Catherine Regina, College of Mount St. Vincent; Angela Cave, Manhattanville College; Sister Mary Charles, i.h.m., Immaculata College; Irene Chayes, Hollins College; Dorothy Christie, Dutchess Community College; John A. Christie, Vassar College; Sister Mary Chrysostom, College of Mount St. Vincent; Mother Madeleine Clary, o.s.u., College of New Rochelle; James L. Clifford, Columbia University; Emily Cloyd, Mt. Holyoke College; William Coley, Wesleyan University; Arthur Collins, State University College (Albany); John Coolidge, University of California (Berkeley); Mother Madeleine Cooney, Manhattanville College; Roberta Cornelius, Randolph-Macon Woman's College; G. Armour Craig, Amherst College; Martha Craig, Wellesley College; Clyde Craine, University of Detroit; Lucille Crighton, Gulf Park College; John Curry, s.j., LeMoyne College (Syracuse); Elizabeth Daniels, Vassar College; Marlies Danziger, Hunter College; Charles T. Davis, Pennsylvania State University; Winifred M. Davis, Carl H. Pforzheimer Library; Charlotte D'Evelyn, Mt. Holyoke College; Sister Mary Aquinas Devlin, Rosary College; John Dorenkamp, College of the Holy Cross; Marjorie Downing, Sarah Lawrence College; Edgar G. Duncan, Vanderbilt University; Mrs. Edgar Duncan; Mother Margaret Mary Dunn, Manhattanville College; Owen Duston, Wabash College; Benjamin W. Early, Mary Washington College,

University of Virginia; Edward Easton, Pace College; Sister Elizabeth Marian, College of Mount St. Vincent; Scott Elledge, Cornell University; Richard Ellmann, Northwestern University; William Elton, University of California (Riverside); Martha Winburn England, Queens College; David V. Erdman, New York Public Library; Sister Mary Eugene, College of Mount St. Vincent; Sister Marie Eugénie, i.h.m., Immaculata College; Mother Mary Robert Falls, o.s.u., College of New Rochelle; Arthur Fenner, Catholic University; P. D. Fleck, University of Western Ontario (Canada); Avron Fleischman, Hofstra College; Edward Fletcher, University of Texas; F. Cudworth Flint, Dartmouth College; Sister Florence Marie, o.p., Caldwell College for Women; Claude Flory, Florida State University; Martha Fodaski, Brooklyn College; Richard Fogle, Tulane University; Stephen Fogle, University of Florida; George Ford, University of Rochester; Elizabeth Foster, Oberlin College; Frances Foster, Vassar College; Robert W. Frank, Jr., Pennsylvania State University; Albert Friedman, Claremont Graduate School; Norman Friedman, University of Connecticut; William Frost, University of California (Santa Barbara); Northrop Frye, Victoria College, University of Toronto (Canada); Paul Fussell, Rutgers State University; Alexander Gelley, C.C.N.Y.; Sister Anne Barbara Gill, Emmanuel College; Walter Goetz, Northwestern University; Malcolm Goldstein, Queens College; Sister Mary Gonzaga, r.s.m., Maria College; Anthony Gosse, Bucknell University; Harvey Granite, University of Rochester; John Grant, University of Connecticut; James Gray, Bishop's University (Canada); Helen Greany, Columbia University; Stanley Gutin, Wilkes College; Husain Haddawy, Wesleyan University; Jean Hagstrum, Northwestern University; Mrs. Hallberg Haldmundson, Queens College; Lawrence Hall, Bowdoin College; Robert Halsband, Columbia University; John Harcourt, Ithaca College; James Harrison, Chicago 10, Ill.; John Hart, Carnegie Institute of Technology; Ann

Louise Hayes, Carnegie Institute of Technology; Allen T. Hazen, Columbia University; Thelma Henner, Columbia University; Neil Hertz, Cornell University; William Hill, s.j., Novitiate of St. Isaac Jogues; Mark Hillegas, Colgate University; W. D. Hirsch, Yale University; B. Hochman, S.U. Maritime College (Fort Schuyler); Daniel Hoffman, Swarthmore College; Jill Hoffman, Cornell University; Stanley Holberg, St. Lawrence University; Norman Holland, Massachusetts Institute of Technology; John Hollander, Yale University; Vivian Hopkins, State University College (Albany); Muriel Hughes, University of Vermont; J. Paul Hunter, Williams College; Samuel Hynes, Swarthmore College, Julia Hysham, Skidmore College; Sister Jeanne Pierre, c.s.j., College of St. Rose; Wilfred Jewkes, Pennsylvania State University; Richard Johnson, Cornell University; Leonidas Jones, University of Vermont; George Kahrl, Elmira College; R. J. Kaufman, University of Rochester; Seana Keen, Vassar College; Cornelia Kelley, University of Illinois; Robert Kellogg, University of Virginia; Edith Kern, St. John's University; Karl Kiralis, St. Lawrence University; Clara Kirk, Douglass College; H. L. Kleinfield, C. W. Post College; Carl Klinck, University of Western Ontario (Canada); Mary Knapp, Western College for Women; Henry Knepler, Illinois Institute of Technology; Edwin Knowles, Pratt Institute; Karl Kroeber, University of Wisconsin; Craig LaDrière, Catholic University; John Lahey, s.j., LeMoyne College (Syracuse); Seymour Lainoff, Yeshiva College; Henry Lavin, s.j., Loyola College (Baltimore); C. Eugene Law, f.s.c., Manhattan College; Lewis Leary, Columbia University; Gaylord LeRoy, Temple University; George Levine, Northwestern University; Oswald LeWinter, Pennsylvania State University; Leon Lewis, College of the Holy Cross; R. W. B. Lewis, Yale University; Ellen Leyburn, Agnes Scott College; Dwight Lindley, Hamilton College; Winslow Loveland, Boston University; Joseph Lovering, Canisius

College; Judson Lyon, State University College (New Paltz); Marion Mabey, Wells College; William McBrien, St. John's University; Rev. Adrian J. McCarthy, University of Dayton; Leonard McCarthy, s.j., College of the Holy Cross; John McChesney, Hotchkiss School; Mrs. Thomas McDade, Manhattanville College; Richard Macksey, Johns Hopkins University; Hugh MacLean, York University (Canada); Jay MacPherson, Victoria College, University of Toronto (Canada); Mother C. E. Maguire, College of the Sacred Heart (Newton); Mother Marie-Louise, o.s.u., New Rochelle; Harold Martin, Harvard University; Louis Martz, Yale University; John K. Mathison, University of Wyoming; Merrill May, Purdue University; Richard McM. Meara, Drury College; Donald C. Mell, Rutgers State University; Paul Memmo, Fordham University; Vivian Mercier, C.C.N.Y.; Harrison T. Meserole, Pennsylvania State University; John Middendorf, Columbia University; Mother Grace Monahan, o.s.u., College of New Rochelle; Julian Moynahan, Princeton University; William Nelson, Columbia University; George Nesbitt, Hamilton College; Helaine Newstead, Hunter College; Eleanor Nicholes, Harvard University; William T. Noon, s.j., Loyola Seminary of Fordham University; Mother Mary Norbert, Rosemont College; Gertrude E. Noyes, Connecticut College; Robert O'Clair, Manhattanville College; Mother E. O'Gorman, Manhattanville College; Gerald O'Grady, Rice University; Joseph O'Neill, s.j., Fordham University; Ants Oras, University of Florida; James M. Osborn, Yale University; Ward Pafford, Emory University; George B. Parks, Queens College; Edward Partridge, Bucknell University; Sister Mary Paton, r.s.m., Saint Xavier College; Roy Harvey Pearce, Ohio State University; Norman Holmes Pearson, Yale University; Frederick Plotkin, Columbia University; Henry Popkin, New York University; Lee H. Potter, George Mason College, University of Virginia; Abbie F. Potts, Rockford College; Irwin Primer, Rutgers State University

(Newark); William Pritchard, Amherst College; E. Jean Protheroe, Hope College; Max Putzel, University of Connecticut; Warren Ramsey, University of California (Berkeley); Helen Randall, Smith College; Isabel Rathbone, Hunter College; Robert Raymo, Rutgers State University (Newark); Elizabeth Revell, University of Western Ontario (Canada); Warner G. Rice, University of Michigan; Mary L. Rion, Agnes Scott College; Sister Rita Margaret, o. p., Caldwell College for Women; Francis X. Roellinger, Oberlin College; Franklin R. Rogers, University of Wisconsin (Milwaukee); H. B. Rouse, University of Arkansas; Rebecca Ruggles, Brooklyn College; Richard Sáez, Yale University; Mother M. Saito, r.s.c.j., International University of the Sacred Heart (Tokyo); Henry Sams, Pennsylvania State University; Irene Samuel, Hunter College; C. Earle Sanborn, University of Western Ontario (Canada); Gennaro Santangelo, Harpur College; Bernard V. Schilling, University of Rochester; Howard Schless, Columbia University; Helen Schnabel, New York 40; Elisabeth Schneider, Temple University; Robert Scholes, University of Virginia; Flora Rheta Schreiber, The New School; Merton Sealts, Lawrence College; Richard Sexton, Fordham University; Ernest Sirluck, University College, University of Toronto (Canada); William Sloane, Dickinson College; Nolan E. Smith, Yale University; Thomas Smith, Duquesne University; Nelle Smither, Douglass College; Monroe K. Spears, University of the South; George Stade, Columbia University; Emily Stanley, University of Connecticut (Hartford); Sister Stephanie, Albertus Magnus College; Sister Mary Stephen, Trinity College (Washington, D.C.); Martha Stone, University of Maryland; Maureen Sullivan, Albertus Magnus College; Stanley Sultan, Clark University; Edward Surtz, s.j., Loyola University (Chicago); James Sutherland, University College (London, England); Barbara Swain, Vassar College; Victor Swain, University of Bridgeport; Anne Ross Taylor, Brown University; Ruth Z. Temple,

Brooklyn College; E. W. Terwilliger, Ithaca College; Sister Therese, Trinity College (Washington, D.C.); Mrs. Clara Thomas, York University (Canada); Wright Thomas, State University College (Cortland); Mother Thomas Aquinas, o.s.u., College of New Rochelle; Doris Thompson, Russell Saga College; Rachel Trickett, St. Hugh's College, Oxford University (England); Susan Turner, Vassar College; S. O. A. Ullman, Union College; Eugene B. Vest, University of Illinois (Navy Pier); Howard Vincent, Kent State University; Sister M. Vincentia, o.p., Albertus Magnus College; Eugene M. Waith, Yale University; Andrew Walker, Georgia Institute of Technology; Aileen Ward, Sarah Lawrence College; René Wellek, Yale University; Philip Wheelwright, University of California (Riverside); Mother Elizabeth White, College of the Sacred Heart (Newton); Joseph Wiesenfarth, F.s.c., LaSalle College; Mother Margaret Williams, Manhattanville College; John H. Wilson, College of the Holy Cross; W. K. Wimsatt, Yale University; Calhoun Winton, University of Delaware; Carl Woodring, Columbia University; Samuel Workman, Newark College of Engineering; Vianney Wormwald, o.f.m., Siena College; Mabel Worthington, Temple University; Philip Yedinsky, Drexel Institute; William Youngren, Massachusetts Institute of Technology; Curt Zimansky, University of Iowa.